W9-BWF-333

921
HAM
c.1

Hamer

921
HAM
c.1 Rubel, David
Fannie Lou Hamer   13.75

DATE DUE	BORROWER'S NAME	
2-21st	Kellyva yhnbra	263
	Shaquota	

FANNIE LOU HAMER

From Sharecropping to Politics

The History of the
Civil Rights Movement

FANNIE LOU HAMER

From Sharecropping to Politics

by *David Rubel*

With an Introduction by

ANDREW YOUNG

Silver Burdett Press

921
H

To my grandmother, also a determined woman

I would like to thank June Johnson for her invaluable contribution to this book, and Howard Schless for giving me a B+ when I clearly deserved an A−.

Series Consultant: Aldon Morris

Cover and Text Design: Design Five, New York
Maps: General Cartography, Inc.
Series Editorial Supervisor: Richard G. Gallin
Series Supervision of Art and Design: Leslie Bauman
Series Editing: Agincourt Press
Concept Editor: Della Rowland

Consultants: Jessie B. Gladden, Division Specialist, Office of Social Studies, Baltimore City Schools, Baltimore, Maryland; Fath Ruffins, Historian, National Museum of American History, Smithsonian Institution, Washington, D.C.

Library of Congress Cataloging-in-Publication Data

Rubel, David.
   Fannie Lou Hamer: from sharecropping to politics / by David Rubel.
      p.   cm. —(The History of the civil rights movement)
   Includes bibliographical references and index.
   Summary: Follows the life of one of the first black organizers of voter registration in Mississippi.
   1. Hamer, Fannie Lou—Juvenile literature. 2. Afro-Americans—Biography—Juvenile literature. 3. Civil rights workers—United States—Biography—Juvenile literature. 4. Afro-Americans—Civil rights—Juvenile literature. 5. Civil rights movements—United States—History—20th century—Juvenile literature. 6. Sharecropping—Mississippi—History—20th century—Juvenile literature. 7. Mississippi—Rural conditions—Juvenile literature. [1. Hamer, Fannie Lou. 2. Civil rights workers. 3. Afro-Americans—Biography.] I. Title. II. Series.
E185.97.H35R83   1990
973'.049607302—dc20
[B]   90-31789
                                                                          CIP
                                                                           AC
ISBN 0-382-09923-0 (lib bdg.)
      0-382-24061-8 (pbk.)

CONTENTS

INTRODUCTION

By Andrew Young

Some thirty years ago, a peaceful revolution took place in the United States, as African Americans sought equal rights. That revolution, which occurred between 1954 and 1968, is called the civil rights movement. Actually, African Americans have been struggling for their civil rights for as long as they have been in this country. Before the Civil War, brave abolitionists were calling out for an end to the injustice and cruelty of slavery. Even after the Civil War freed slaves, African Americans were still forced to fight other forms of racism and discrimination—segregation and prejudice. This movement still continues today as people of color battle racial hatred and economic exploitation all over the world.

The books in this series tell the stories of the lives of Ella Baker, Stokely Carmichael, Fannie Lou Hamer, Jesse Jackson, Malcolm X, Thurgood Marshall, Rosa Parks, A. Philip Randolph, and Martin Luther King, Jr.—just a few of the thousands of brave people who worked in the civil rights movement. Learning about these heroes is an important lesson in American history. They risked their homes and their jobs—and some gave their lives—to secure rights and freedoms that we now enjoy and often take for granted.

Most of us know the name of Dr. Martin Luther King, Jr., the nonviolent leader of the movement. But others who were just as important may not be as familiar. Rosa Parks insisted on her right to a seat on a public bus. Her action started a bus boycott that changed a segregation law and sparked a movement.

Ella Baker was instrumental in founding two major civil rights organizations, the Southern Christian Leadership Conference (SCLC) and the Student Nonviolent Coordinating Committee (SNCC). One of the chairpersons of SNCC, Stokely Carmichael, is perhaps best known for making the slogan "Black Power" famous. Malcolm X, the strong voice from the urban north, rose from a prison inmate to a powerful black Muslim leader.

Not many people know that the main organizer of the 1963 March on Washington was A. Philip Randolph. Younger leaders called Randolph the "father of the movement." Fannie Lou Hamer, a poor sharecropper from Mississippi, was such a powerful speaker for voters rights that President Lyndon Johnson blocked out television coverage of the 1964 Democratic National Convention to keep her off the air. Thurgood Marshall was the first African American to be made a Supreme Court justice.

Many who demanded equality paid for their actions. They were fired from their jobs, thrown out of their homes, beaten, and even killed. But they marched, went to jail, and put their lives on the line over and over again for the right to equal justice. These rights include something as simple as being able to sit and eat at a lunch counter. They include political rights such as the right to vote. They also include the equal rights to education and job opportunities that lead to economic betterment.

We are now approaching a level of democracy that allows all citizens of the United States to participate in the American dream. Jesse Jackson, for example, has pursued the dream of the highest office in this land, the president of the United States. Jackson's running for president was made possible by those who went before him. They are the people whose stories are included in this biography and history series, as well as thousands of others who remain nameless. They are people who depend upon you to carry on the dream of liberty and justice for all people of the world.

Civil Rights Movement Time Line

—1954———1955———1956———1957—

May 17—
Brown v. Board of Education of Topeka I: Supreme Court rules racial segregation in public is unconstitutional.

May 31—
Brown v. Board of Education of Topeka II: Supreme Court says desegregation of public schools must proceed "with all deliberate speed."

August 28—
14-year-old Emmett Till is killed in Money, Mississippi.

December 5, 1955–December 20, 1956—
Montgomery, Alabama bus boycott.

November 13—
Supreme Court outlaws racial segregation on Alabama's city buses.

January 10, 11—
Southern Christian Leadership Conference (SCLC) is founded.

August 29—
Civil Rights Act is passed. Among other things, it creates Civil Rights Commission to advise the president and gives government power to uphold voting rights.

September 1957–
Little Rock Central High School is desegregated.

—1962———1963———1964—

September 29—
Federal troops help integrate University of Mississippi ("Ole Miss") after two people are killed and several are injured.

April to May—
Birmingham, Alabama, demonstrations. School children join the marches.

May 20—
Supreme Court rules Birmingham's segregation laws are unconstitutional.

June 12—
NAACP worker Medgar Evers is killed in Jackson, Mississippi.

August 28—
March on Washington draws more than 250,000 people.

September 15—
Four girls are killed when a Birmingham church is bombed.

November 22—
President John F. Kennedy is killed in Dallas, Texas.

March–June—
St. Augustine, Florida, demonstrations.

June 21—
James Chaney, Michael Schwerner, and Andrew Goodman are killed while registering black voters in Mississippi.

July 2—
Civil Rights Act is passed. Among other things, it provides for equal job opportunities and gives the government power to sue to desegregate public schools and facilities.

August—
Mississippi Freedom Democratic Party (MFDP) attempts to represent Mississippi at the Democratic National Convention.

1958 — 1959 — 1960 — 1961

September 1958–August 1959—
Little Rock Central High School is closed because governor refuses to integrate it.

February 1—
Student sit-ins at lunch counter in Greensboro, North Carolina, begin sit-in protests all over the South.

April 17—
Student Nonviolent Coordinating Committee (SNCC) is founded.

May 6—
Civil Rights Act is passed. Among other things, it allows judges to appoint people to help blacks register to vote.

Eleven African countries win their independence.

May 4—
Freedom Rides leave Washington, D.C., and head south.

September 22—
Interstate Commerce Commission ordered to enforce desegregation laws on buses, and trains, and in travel facilities like waiting rooms, rest rooms, and restaurants.

1965 — 1966 — 1967 — 1968

January–March—
Selma, Alabama, demonstrations.

February 21—
Malcolm X is killed in New York City.

March 21–25—
More than 25,000 march from Selma to Montgomery, Alabama.

August 6—
Voting Rights Act passed.

August 11–16—
Watts riot (Los Angeles, California).

June—
James Meredith "March Against Fear" from Memphis, Tennessee, to Jackson, Mississippi. Stokely Carmichael makes slogan "Black Power" famous during march.

Fall—
Black Panther Party for Self-Defense is formed by Huey Newton and Bobby Seale in Oakland, California.

June 13—
Thurgood Marshall is appointed first African-American U.S. Supreme Court justice.

Summer—
Riots break out in 30 U.S. cities.

April 4—
Martin Luther King, Jr., is killed in Memphis, Tennessee.

April 11—
Civil Rights Act is passed. Among other things, it prohibits discrimination in selling and renting houses or apartments.

May 13–June 23—
Poor People's March: Washington, D.C., to protest poverty.

1 GO TELL IT ON THE MOUNTAIN

66 *If the Freedom Democratic Party is not seated now, I question America. Is this America, the land of the free and the home of the brave, where we have to sleep with our telephones off of the hook because our lives be threatened daily, because we want to live as decent human beings in America?* **99**

FANNIE LOU HAMER before the Democratic National Convention, 1964

In August 1964, the Democratic party held its national convention in Atlantic City, New Jersey. Attending the convention were delegates from all over the country. Usually at a national party convention, each state has its own group of delegates. But at the 1964 Democratic convention, the state of Mississippi had two delegations.

One was made up of whites only. These delegates were known as the "regulars" because they had been running the Mississippi Democratic party for as long as anyone could remember. The white regulars stood for segregation in the South, which was the system that kept blacks apart from whites.

Segregation kept blacks from using white-only water fountains, eating at white-only restaurants, and attending white-only schools, which were always much better than the schools set up for blacks. In fact, the Mississippi Democratic party was itself segregated. It did not allow blacks to participate or to vote.

The delegation that challenged the white-only regulars was made up of both blacks and whites. It was called the Mississippi Freedom Democratic Party (MFDP). It was organized so that black citizens could have a say in how they were governed.

The vice-chairman of the MFDP was Fannie Lou Hamer of Ruleville, Mississippi, a small town in the northern part of the state. As in much of rural Mississippi, most of the poor in Ruleville were black, and most of the blacks were poor. Hamer was both poor and black, but still she had come to Atlantic City, so far from her home, to fight for her rights and those of her neighbors.

During the summer of 1964, both the white regulars and the MFDP had held local elections, called precinct caucuses, and state conventions to choose their delegates to the national convention. All the citizens of Mississippi were invited to participate in the MFDP caucuses. Only whites were allowed to participate in the caucuses of the regular Mississippi Democratic party.

Because each Mississippi party had held elections, both claimed to represent the people of the state. But according to the rules of the Democratic party, only one state party could have its delegates seated at the national convention.

Before the convention opened in Atlantic City, most people had thought it would be a boring one. There was only one serious candidate for president, Lyndon Baines Johnson of

Texas. It was certain that he would get the nomination. Also, it was well known that Senator Hubert Humphrey of Minnesota would be his vice-presidential running mate.

But people who thought the convention would be boring had not counted on Fannie Lou Hamer. With one short, nationally televised speech before the convention, Hamer did what newspaper stories and secondhand accounts had been unable to do. She brought the hard reality of black life in the South into clear focus for every American watching at home. She gave that suffering a human face.

Over the years, many words have been used to refer to Americans of African descent—*Negro, colored, people of color, black*, and *African American*. Depending on how each was used, it could be insulting, or it could reflect pride. Beyond these words, however, has always been the reality that African Americans have suffered throughout this nation's history.

The story of suffering that Fannie Lou Hamer told the Democratic convention in 1964 was her own, but it was also the story of thousands of others who never made it to Atlantic City. Some didn't come because they were too scared. Others didn't come because they were dead.

The Atlantic City convention was an important one for Lyndon Johnson. Four years earlier, in 1960, the Democrats had nominated John F. Kennedy for president, and Lyndon Johnson had been Kennedy's running mate. When Kennedy won the election and became president, Johnson became his vice president. Then when Kennedy was shot and killed in Dallas on November 22, 1963, Johnson became president.

Now President Johnson wanted to win reelection. He felt that it was important for the Democratic party to unite behind him. He wanted no surprises at the convention. He tried to manage it so that controversial issues would be avoided. The claims of the MFDP, however, were very controversial.

What the MFDP wanted sounds simple: it wanted African Americans to be able to vote and help choose the officials who governed them. This was the American way, after all. But it was far from simple.

The difficulty went back to the end of the Civil War, when the slaves were freed. The years immediately following the Civil War were the first period of progress for African Americans in the South. In history books, that period has become known as Reconstruction. In 1870, the 15th Amendment to the Constitution gave African Americans the right to vote. (Until 1920, women of whatever race did not have the right to vote in national elections.) During Reconstruction, African Americans voted in surprisingly large numbers. Between 1869 and 1877, for example, 16 African Americans were elected to Congress from the South, including two senators from Mississippi.

But by 1877 voting by blacks began to drop off. Because southern whites feared the power of large numbers of black voters, they began to pass new laws in the state legislatures. These laws made it difficult, if not impossible, for poor blacks to vote.

One popular method used to stop blacks from voting was the poll tax. This was a tax paid by everyone who voted. Because most blacks in the South were very poor, they could not afford to pay the tax. Therefore, they could not vote.

Another method used against blacks was the literacy test. All voters had to take the test to prove that they could read. But most blacks were given a much harder test than whites.

Finally, if both the poll tax and the literacy tax failed, then some whites used tougher measures. Blacks were beaten, and even murdered, to keep them from voting. As a result, voting by blacks slowed to a trickle. As late as 1896, there were 130,000 blacks registered to vote in Louisiana. By 1904, only 1,342 were registered.

In Mississippi, where Fannie Lou Hamer lived, there were almost one million African-American residents in 1963, but only 28,000 of them were registered voters. The MFDP's goal was to change things so that Mississippi's blacks could exercise their political rights in the same way that whites did. Only by

Highlights in the Life of Fannie Lou Hamer

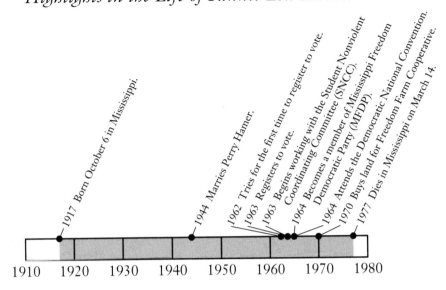

1917 Born October 6 in Mississippi.

1944 Marries Perry Hamer.

1962 Tries for the first time to register to vote.

1963 Registers to vote.

1963 Begins working with the Student Nonviolent Coordinating Committee (SNCC).

1964 Becomes a member of Mississippi Freedom Democratic Party (MFDP).

1964 Attends the Democratic National Convention.

1970 Buys land for Freedom Farm Cooperative.

1977 Dies in Mississippi on March 14.

1910   1920   1930   1940   1950   1960   1970   1980

voting, MFDP leaders felt, could blacks in the South truly obtain justice.

At the Atlantic City convention, the 108-member Credentials Committee, which was controlled by President Johnson's people, had the power to decide who would and who would not be seated. On August 22, a Saturday afternoon, the MFDP presented its case to the Credentials Committee.

The hearing was televised nationally, so that people all over the country could watch and learn about what life in the South was like for African Americans. Millions tuned in.

Most of the best known leaders of the civil rights movement appeared to testify before the Credentials Committee. Martin Luther King, Jr., of the Southern Christian Leadership Conference (SCLC), testified. James Farmer, of the Congress of Racial Equality (CORE), testified. So did Roy Wilkins, of the National Association for the Advancement of Colored People (NAACP). Each of these men was well educated, well spoken, and nationally known. Then it was time for Fannie Lou Hamer to speak. Hamer was neither well educated nor famous. She was a poor plantation worker from a small town in Mississippi who had never been allowed to vote in her life and had never attended school past the sixth grade.

Fannie Lou Hamer testifies before 1964 Democratic National Convention in Atlantic City.

Yet it is Fannie Lou Hamer's testimony that is remembered today. And it was Fannie Lou Hamer's story, more than anyone else's, that made white Americans aware of the hardships faced by southern blacks.

King had already spoken when the MFDP lawyer, Joseph Rauh, presented Hamer to the Credentials Committee. The year before, she had been arrested in Winona, Mississippi, for trying to eat in a white-only restaurant. This is what she told the committee that day, on national television, about her arrest:

> I was carried to the county jail and...placed in a cell with...Miss Euvester Simpson. After I was placed in the cell, I began to hear sounds of licks and screams. I could hear the sounds of licks and horrible screams. And I could hear somebody say, "Can you say 'Yes, sir,' nigger? Can you say 'Yes, sir'?"
> And they would say other horrible names.

[Miss Annelle Ponder] would say, "Yes, I can say 'Yes, sir.'"

"So say it."

She says, "I don't know you well enough."

They beat her, I don't know how long, and after awhile she began to pray and asked God to have mercy on these people.

And it wasn't too long before three white men came to my cell. . . .

I was carried out of the cell into another cell where they had two Negro prisoners. The state highway patrolman ordered the first Negro to take the blackjack.

The first Negro prisoner ordered me, by orders from the state highway patrolman, to lay down on a bunk bed on my face, and I laid on my face.

The first Negro began to beat and I was beat until he was exhausted. . . . After the first Negro . . . was exhausted, the state highway patrolman ordered the second Negro to take the blackjack. The second Negro began to beat and I began to work my feet, and the state highway patrolman ordered the first Negro who had beat to set on my feet and keep me from working my feet. I began to scream, and one white man got up and began to beat me on my head and tell me to "hush."

Fannie Lou Hamer was very nearly killed that day, simply for entering a restaurant. But even this severe beating did not stop her from continuing her efforts on behalf of all African Americans. She received constant threats of harm to herself and her family, but her presence in Atlantic City alone proved her exceptional moral courage.

Her presence there also demonstrated her great passion for the cause of civil rights, a passion not unlike that she felt for her deep Christian faith. Her speech at the convention was especially moving because when Fannie Lou Hamer spoke, she spoke from the heart and she spoke from the soul.

Long before Hamer became one of the few women leaders of a

Fannie Lou Hamer leads other MFDP delegates in a freedom song. On her left is activist Ella Baker.

national movement, she had been preaching the Gospel and singing songs of freedom and salvation. When Hamer spoke, you could hear the sound of her faith echoing way down inside her.

"If the Freedom Democratic Party is not seated now," Hamer told the Credentials Committee in a voice that sounded as though she was reading from the Bible, "I question America. Is this America, the land of the free and the home of the brave, where we have to sleep with our telephones off of the hook because our lives be threatened daily, because we want to live as decent human beings in America?"

This was 1964. Americans thought they lived in a modern, democratic society. But many who heard Fannie Lou Hamer on television that day began to wonder whether or not America really did stand for justice and democracy.

Out of the deepest backwaters of Mississippi, Fannie Lou Hamer had risen to tell them something. And that day, they listened, some for the first time.

Was this really America?

INTO THE FIELDS

> **"** *I really didn't know who to make a promise to. And I just really asked God, because I believe in God, I asked God to give me a chance to just let me do something about what was going on in Mississippi.* **"**

FANNIE LOU HAMER, speaking of her childhood in Ruleville

Fannie Lou Hamer was born on October 6, 1917, and she grew up in a tar-paper shack, sleeping on a cotton sack stuffed with dry grass under a roof patched up with tin. When she was two years old, her family moved to Sunflower County, where Hamer lived for the rest of her life.

Her father was Jim Townsend; her mother, Lou Ella. Even by Mississippi standards, the Townsend family was a large one: 14 boys and 6 girls. Fannie Lou was the 20th child.

Like most of the poor African-American families in rural Mississippi, the Townsends were sharecroppers. During the growing season, they would plant and pick cotton, giving half their crop to the plantation boss, who owned the land on which the cotton was grown. This practice was called sharecropping because the farmers had to "share" their crops. It was also called halving. Either way, it was difficult for sharecroppers to make enough money to live because they could keep only half of what they had grown.

Back before the Civil War, before the slaves were freed, southern plantations were run with slave labor. Cotton, often called "King Cotton," was the most important crop, and it required a lot of workers to grow and to harvest. Many southern plantation owners became rich because they had slaves to supply that labor at a very low cost.

Once the slaves were freed, however, the plantation owners lost their cheap labor. This threatened the whole economy of the South. For the plantation owner, the solution to this problem was sharecropping.

Sharecropping was a terrible way of life for the freed slaves. However, they were poorly educated and desperately in need of work. There was little else most of them could do.

As sharecroppers, African Americans were no longer slaves, but their lives were not much better. They were still breaking their backs picking cotton, and they were still poor. It was very difficult to get ahead. Under the system of sharecropping, the cost of seed, fertilizer, and other supplies all came out of the sharecropper's half. Most families, parents and children alike, had to work 12 to 14 hours a day just to stay alive.

Fannie Lou Hamer grew up amid this hardship. She first went down into the fields when she was six years old. This is how she remembers that day:

> I can remember very well the landowner telling me one day that if I would pick thirty pounds [of cotton], he would give me something out of the commissary: some Crackerjacks, Daddy-Wide-Legs [a gingerbread cookie], and some sar-

A young man picks cotton in an Arkansas field.

dines. These were things that I knew I loved and never had a chance to have. So I picked thirty pounds that day. Well, the next week I had to pick sixty and by the time I was thirteen, I was picking two and three hundred pounds.

Children such as Fannie Lou were often hungry, so it was easy to trick them into proving they were old enough to work. In this way, the plantation owners could get extra workers. They knew that no sharecropping family could afford to let a pair of useful hands lie idle. It did not matter whether they were the hands of a child or not.

The commissary, or company store, to which the landowner took the young Fannie Lou was another trick. The company store gave credit to all the plantation workers so that they could buy the supplies they needed to grow cotton and to live. But the prices the company store charged were so high that the workers were always in debt. And as long as they were in debt, they could never afford to leave the plantation. It was almost like being a slave again.

The sharecroppers really had no choice. They had to grow cotton to make a living, and they had to buy supplies to grow cotton. Because they had no money, they had to use their credit at the company store.

In his famous novel *The Grapes of Wrath*, John Steinbeck tells of California during the Great Depression. These people, too, were trapped by the company store. And the same thing happened to coal miners in West Virginia.

In all of these cases, it was almost impossible for the workers to earn enough money in any one year to break the cycle of poverty and dependence. By the end of each year, the workers were nearly always in debt.

But if sharecropping was bad for poor blacks, it was very good for the white landowners. Besides providing a cheap work force, sharecropping was also a way to control blacks. Through sharecropping and through denial of the right to vote, whites in the South were able to keep poor blacks down.

Sometimes, if a family worked very hard and had a little luck, it could save enough money to buy its way off the plantation. But even this usually worked against the black sharecroppers. Many whites feared blacks, and were content only when the blacks were kept powerless. In Mississippi particularly, blacks who tried to get ahead in life often received a late-night visit from a white racist group such as the Ku Klux Klan. Their houses were burned, and their lives were threatened. Many blacks were murdered simply for wanting a better life.

As hard as sharecropping was, however, the Townsend family did rather well. After all, 22 pairs of hands can pick quite a lot of cotton. In a good year, Fannie Lou's family could grow and pick 70 bales. (There are 500 pounds of cotton in each bale.)

The year that Fannie Lou turned 12 was one of those good years. The crop came in so well that Jim Townsend was able to save up enough money to rent some land of his own. He even had enough money left over to buy some farm animals, and to fix up the house that came with the land.

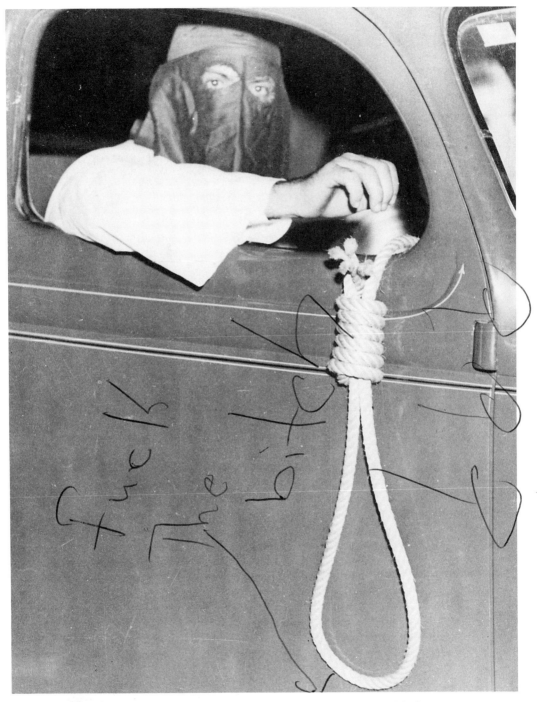

Hooded members of the Ku Klux Klan would often come for blacks in the middle of the night.

"We were doing pretty well," Hamer remembered later. But this upset some of the family's white neighbors. "One night," Hamer continued, "this white man went to our lot, and went to the trough where all the mules had to eat, and stirred up a gallon of Paris Green into the mules' food."

Paris Green is a bright green powder containing arsenic, which is a powerful poison. It's used to kill insects on crops, but it killed the mules just as well.

"It killed everything we had," Hamer said later. "When we got there, one mule was already dead. The other two mules and the cow had their stomachs all swelled up. It was too late to save them. That poison knocked us right back down flat. We never did get back up again."

The Townsends knew what had happened. "That white man did it just because we were getting somewhere," Hamer went on. "White people never like to see Negroes get a little success. All of this is not secret in the state of Mississippi."

The poisoning forced the family back onto the plantation. Now they were even worse off than before.

Until this time, Fannie Lou had been going to school. For the children of sharecroppers, the school year in the South was only four months long: December, January, February, and March. Those were the same four months that children weren't needed to help their families in the fields.

At school, Fannie Lou learned to read and write. She studied hard, and even taught her mother how to write her own name. But with the family suffering such hard times, Fannie Lou had to quit school after the sixth grade.

She kept up her education, though, by joining the Stranger's Home Baptist Church. This gave her the opportunity to read the Bible regularly with others. It also began what became a lifelong involvement with the church.

Times were very hard for Fannie Lou then, even harder for her as a teenager than they had been for her as a child. To get by during the winter months, for example, after the harvest was over, her family had to go from plantation to plantation, asking to pick over fields in case any cotton had been left behind. This was called "scrapping" cotton. Here is how Hamer later described it:

> When [the landowners] would tell [my mother] that we could have the cotton, we would walk for miles and miles and miles in the run of a week. We wouldn't have on shoes or anything because we didn't have them. She would al-

ways tie our feet up with rags because the ground would be froze real hard.

    We would walk from field to field until we had scrapped a bale of cotton. Then she'd take the bale of cotton and sell it, and that would give us some of the food that we would need.

Lou Ella Townsend was a strong and determined woman. She would also go from house to house and help slaughter hogs. The people she helped would then give her the intestines of the pig, and sometimes also the feet and the head.

    According to Hamer, "Things like that helped keep us going." Many times during those winters the Townsends would have nothing for dinner but greens without seasoning and flour gravy. "My mother would mix flour with a little grease and try to make gravy out of it," recalled Hamer, but "sometimes there'd be nothing to eat but bread and onions."

These were the years of the Great Depression, a time of hardship for many Americans. The depression began with the stock market crash of 1929, in which companies went bankrupt and many families lost all their money. The economy was in such trouble that many people were thrown out of work.

Hamer always respected her mother most of all for helping the family to pull through these tough times. She said:

> My mother was a great woman. She went through a lot of suffering to bring the twenty of us up, but still she taught us to be decent and to respect ourselves, and that is one of the things that has kept me going. . . .
>
> At the beginning of my young life I wanted to be white. The reason was that we worked every day, hard work, and we never did have food. The people that wasn't working, which was the white folks, they had food and they had clothes and everything. So I wanted to be white.
>
> I asked my mother one time [when I was around ten] why I wasn't white, so that we could have some food. She told me, "Don't ever, ever say that again. Don't feel like that. We are not bad because we're black people."
>
> And it wasn't many weeks passed that she wouldn't tell me, "You respect yourself as a black child. And when you're grown, if I'm dead and gone, you respect yourself as a black woman, and other people will respect you."

In later years, Hamer remembered how she used to work with her mother on crews that were clearing the land around Sunflower County. Lou Ella Townsend would chop down brush and trees with an ax, just as the men did. Then Fannie Lou would rake up the brush and burn it.

While working on one of these crews, Mrs. Townsend had a serious accident. A splinter from a tree she was chopping down flew up and stuck in her eye. Unable to get the proper medical care, Lou Ella Townsend slowly began to lose her sight. Near the end of her life, she was almost totally blind.

Fannie Lou knew that her parents had given all they could in order to clear the land of Sunflower County. That's why it saddened her to see that they could not share equally in its bounty. "The same land that's in cultivation now," she would say, "they got closed to us.... We can't own [it, even though] my parents helped to make this ground what it is."

Although it seemed things couldn't get much worse, they did. Jim Townsend had a stroke in 1939. After that, Lou Ella had to take on all of the responsibility for keeping the family together.

Fannie Lou remembered that, as her mother got older, her clothes became heavier and more ragged. As they would tear, Lou Ella Townsend would mend them. And then when the mends tore, she would mend them again.

"I promised myself [that] if I ever got grown, I would never see her wear a patched-patched piece [again]," Hamer said.

All of this suffering made such a strong impression on Fannie Lou as a young woman that she began to make promises to herself, because "I really didn't know who to make a promise to. And I just really asked God, because I believed in God, I asked God to give me a chance to just let me do something about what was going on in Mississippi."

3 LIKE MY MOTHER BEFORE ME

> ❝ *My main object of working was wanting the children to have a better way of living, that the world might be just a little better because the Lord had me here for something. And I tried to make good out of it. That was my aim.* ❞
>
> MAUD LEE BRYANT,
> sharecropper and maid

In 1944, Fannie Lou Townsend married Perry "Pap" Hamer, a tractor driver and sharecropper on a nearby plantation. The plantation was located just outside Ruleville. It was owned by a man named W. D. Marlowe. Marlowe, of course, was white.

For the next 18 years, Fannie Lou Hamer's life was much like that of her mother. She worked in the fields during the day chopping cotton. At night she cleaned the Marlowes' house for some extra money. She was also the plantation's timekeeper. Her job was to keep records of the number of hours each hand worked, the number of bales each one picked, and the amount of pay due each worker.

"We didn't have it easy" is how Hamer described her life then. "The only way we could ever make it through the winter was because Pap had a little juke joint [a saloon] and we made liquor. That was the only way we made it."

Life was much the same for poor African-American women all over the rural South. Maud Lee Bryant was a sharecropper who lived in Moncure, North Carolina. She didn't know Fannie Lou Hamer, but her time was spent in much the same way. Like Hamer, Bryant chopped cotton in the fields during the day and worked in a white man's house at night, scrubbing floors, washing clothes, sewing, and ironing.

"My main object of working," Mrs. Bryant once told an interviewer, "was wanting the children to have a better way of living, that the world might be just a little better because the Lord had me here for something. And I tried to make good out of it. That was my aim."

Often, as with both Bryant and Hamer, it was their religious faith that gave African-American women the strength to endure the hardness of their days.

The truth was that many poor southerners, both black and white, were trapped by sharecropping. Under that unfair system, sharecropping families, like mining families and fruit-picking families, could never earn enough to be independent. The whites who were in charge knew this. In fact, that was the whole point of sharecropping. Wealthy southerners believed that real freedom for blacks was dangerous—dangerous for the whites, that is.

Wealthy southerners also believed that black freedom would end white control of society. They also feared that it would doom the cotton industry, which many whites depended on for their wealth. If blacks couldn't be forced to work for very little money, the white plantation owners would be unable to make a profit.

White plantation owners often made up new rules to keep the blacks down. For instance, if a black family began to raise some hogs for meat, the plantation owner would issue a new rule against raising hogs on the plantation. The sharecroppers were thus forced to buy their pork at the high company-store prices.

Consider this: All her young life, Fannie Lou Hamer had worked in the cotton fields, and still she couldn't afford a new cotton dress. All her life she had worked on a farm, and still she didn't have much to eat. In a novel, this sort of mockery would be called irony. But in the South, it was called life.

Sometimes the difference between the life of a white land-owner and the life of a black sharecropper was made horribly clear. One day when Fannie Lou Hamer was cleaning a bathroom at the Marlowes' house, the Marlowes' daughter told her, "You don't have to clean this one too good. It's just ole Honey's." Honey was the Marlowes' family dog. Pap and Fannie Lou Hamer had to use an outhouse, but the Marlowes' dog had its own indoor bathroom.

All this time, Fannie Lou Hamer felt completely helpless. "I knew it was something wrong," she said, "but I didn't know what to do, and all I could do is rebel in the only way I could rebel."

For most of Fannie Lou Hamer's adult life, rebellion against the system that kept her down meant little more than talking with the other workers in the fields about their common problems. As she said, she didn't know what else to do.

It was the 1940s, and the United States was fighting World War II. The cause of freedom was especially popular in the United States. Americans felt proud that their young men were fighting the evils of Nazi Germany. They were happy to support the cause of freedom abroad.

But Fannie Lou Hamer felt there was something strange about blacks fighting for the United States.

> I said, "You know, the thing that shocked me [was] our people [going] to the Army just like your white people go. And then when they come back home, if they say anything, they killed, they lynched, they murdered."
> I said, "I just don't see no reason they should fight."
> And you know, they looked at me real funny. But I was rebelling in the only way I knew how.

The war years, however, also provided opportunities for both African Americans and women. Because the war economy finally lifted the country out of the Great Depression, jobs were plentiful. These jobs would normally have been filled by white men, but so many of them were away fighting in the army that workers for all the new war-related jobs had to be found elsewhere.

One place these new workers were found was in the kitchen, as many housewives went to work. Another place they were found was down on the plantation.

Though most of the new jobs were located in the industrial cities of the North, many Southern blacks were happy to move and leave the plantation behind. For many African Americans,

World War II provided their first real opportunity to earn regular paychecks. Even so, the move was a drastic one: not only from South to North, but also from the country to the city.

Considering that the economy was booming during those years, African-American salaries were extremely low. But compared to what African Americans had been earning as share-croppers, the paychecks seemed fat indeed, and this taste of success encouraged many African Americans to raise their expectations.

Many blacks became concerned with such issues as discrimination in public housing and prejudice in the workplace. They joined the National Association for the Advancement of Colored People (NAACP) and worked to change things. The discrimination and prejudice had always been there—in fact, the NAACP had been fighting it since 1909. But only with the changes brought about by the war did large numbers of African Americans begin to believe that they could change society.

Some victories had already been won. The greatest of these came in 1941. In that year, President Franklin Roosevelt signed Executive Order Number 8802. This order banned discrimination in employment in government and in the defense industries. For the first time, it was illegal to reject a job applicant because of the color of his or her skin.

Then in 1942, soon after the United States had entered the war, the Congress of Racial Equality (CORE) was formed. CORE's purpose was to fight for a "double victory"—over fascism abroad and over racism at home. Governments such as Germany's were said to be fascist because they were centralized, all-powerful, and allowed no opposition from the people.

The United States proudly thought of itself as a democratic nation during the war years. But, according to CORE and the NAACP, that was simply not true. All American citizens were *not* being treated as equals. Black soldiers were fighting and dying in Europe and in the Pacific to defend the idea of basic civil rights. But as Fannie Lou Hamer knew well, their relatives back home were being denied those same basic rights.

Even the black soldiers themselves had to serve in segregated, second-class units. White officers were in charge of these units, and sometimes they treated German prisoners of war better than black soldiers who served under them.

But all of this activity was happening a world away from the plantations of Mississippi. Nothing there ever seemed to change, except the seasons. The Hamers planted cotton in the spring and picked it in the fall, year after year. And like her mother before her, Fannie Lou Hamer took to raising a family.

After a few years of marriage, the Hamers realized that they couldn't have children of their own, so they adopted two daughters. The first child they took in, Dorothy Jean, was an infant born to a single mother. The second, Virgie Ree, was five months old when she came to the Hamers.

Virgie Ree had been badly burned in a fire, and her natural parents were too poor to give her the attention she needed. The Hamers, however, always treated both children as their own.

All this time, from childhood up through middle age, Fannie Lou Hamer had longed for change. But there didn't seem to be anything she, or anyone else, could do. The weight of the system was too great.

"Sometimes I be working in the fields," Hamer told *Ebony* in 1966, "and I get so tired. I say to the people picking cotton with us, hard as we have to work for nothing, there must be some way we can change this."

By 1962, Hamer had already spent the better part of a lifetime chopping cotton, cleaning her house, cleaning a white man's house, and raising a family. She was 44 years old then and a nobody, and Ruleville was a nowhere place. But she never gave up hope.

4 INTO THE COURTROOMS

> ❝ *When I opened the door, there was a man standing with a pistol in one hand and a flashlight in the other hand. And he asked me did I have two boys there from Chicago. I told him, 'I have.' And he said, 'I wants the boy that done all that talk.'*
>
> *And they march him to the car, and they ask someone there, Was this the boy? And the answer was yes. And they drove toward Money.* ❞
>
> **MOSE WRIGHT, uncle of Emmett Till**

Fannie Lou Hamer longed for change, but it was slow in coming. One reason was that the most respected organization working for racial equality, the National Association for the Advancement of Colored People (NAACP), did its work in the courts. Progress there happened slowly.

The NAACP was founded in 1909 by a group of people—

both black and white—who wanted change. The well-known black historian W. E. B. Du Bois edited the group's journal, *The Crisis*. Other than Du Bois, however, the NAACP's principal officers at that time were white.

The NAACP was supported largely by middle-class African Americans in the cities, not the poorer African Americans in the countryside. The NAACP's main activities were lobbying for political change and fighting legal battles. Its leaders believed that segregation could be changed in the courts.

To achieve its goals, the NAACP set up the Legal Defense Fund. Important Legal Defense Fund lawyers included Jack Greenberg, who was white, and two African Americans, Constance Baker Motley and Thurgood Marshall. Motley later became the first African-American woman appointed to the federal bench. In 1967, President Johnson named Marshall to be the first African-American justice on the Supreme Court.

For many years, the NAACP Legal Defense Fund followed a careful plan. Its goal was to reverse the famous Supreme Court decision *Plessy v. Ferguson* (1896), which upheld the "Jim Crow" laws in the South. These were the laws that kept African Americans segregated and powerless.

In 1890, the state of Louisiana had passed a Jim Crow law segregating train travel. When Homer Plessy, a black, tried to board a railroad car reserved for whites, he was arrested. He later asked the U.S. Supreme Court to decide whether Louisiana's Jim Crow law was constitutional.

The 14th Amendment to the Constitution, passed in 1868, had guaranteed every citizen of the United States equal protection under the law. But in the *Plessy* case, the Supreme Court said that separation was not necessarily a denial of equality. The Court decided that since other railroad cars were available for African Americans to use, the Louisiana law was constitutional. Three years later, in *Cumming v. Richmond County Board of Education* (1899), the Court extended this "separate but equal" thinking to the public schools.

Following these decisions, state governments and private

businesses in the South set up "separate but equal" facilities for African Americans. Soon there were separate public schools, separate hotels, separate bus-station waiting rooms, and even separate public water fountains. Rarely, though, were the black facilities equal to those made available to whites.

The Legal Defense Fund, led by Marshall, had to fight the idea that separate could somehow be equal. Its lawyers worked for years to change the laws that upheld segregation. Along the way, they had some small victories. Perhaps the most important of these was the Texas Law School case. The state of Texas had set up a separate law school for blacks. In 1950, however, the Supreme Court ruled that it was not as good as the state's law school for whites. Therefore, in this case, separate was *not* equal.

Then in 1954 came the Legal Defense Fund's greatest triumph: the *Brown v. Board of Education of Topeka* case, yet another case set in the public schools. With the help of the NAACP, Oliver Brown sued the Board of Education of Topeka, Kansas. He believed that the black public school that his daughter attended was not as good as the white public schools.

At the trial, Thurgood Marshall produced studies that showed that segregation harmed both black and white children. He also argued that grouping people by race violated the 14th Amendment. This last argument was aimed directly at the heart of the *Plessy* decision.

On May 17, 1954, the recently appointed chief justice, Earl Warren, read the Supreme Court's unanimous decision. Completely reversing *Plessy v. Ferguson*, the decision declared that "in the field of public education the doctrine of 'separate but equal' has no place." To separate schoolchildren "solely because of their race," Warren read, "generates a feeling of inferiority as to their status in the community that may affect their hearts and minds in a way unlikely ever to be undone."

The victory was a triumph for the civil rights movement. There was great celebration in the African-American community. But in practical terms, the decision was only a beginning, because nothing would change overnight. For all its power, the Supreme Court couldn't do away with Jim Crow all by itself.

School boards in the South, for example, were slow to integrate schools. Then, as time dragged on, these delays encouraged even more southern racists to resist the changes.

One tragic incident involved a 14-year-old boy from Chicago named Emmett Till. During the summer of 1955, Till went south to visit some relatives in Money, Mississippi, a town in Tallahatchie County, only about 25 miles from Ruleville.

The killing of blacks was nothing new in the South. In the 18 months following the end of World War II in 1945, for example, there were 45 lynchings, in which blacks were hanged by whites without a judge or a trial. Before World War II, in the years when Fannie Lou Hamer's parents were growing up and white racists were in almost total control, thousands of African Americans were lynched. No one really knows how many. But Emmett Till's death was different because of the national attention it received.

On August 28, 1955, Till was passing time with some other boys outside Money's general store. His cousin, Curtis Jones, was playing checkers with an elderly man nearby. It was just another hot, slow afternoon in Mississippi.

In Money, blacks and whites were kept totally apart, but in Chicago, where Till was from, blacks and whites went to school together. Till showed the boys gathered around the stores pictures of himself with white students from his school, girls and boys. He even said that one of the white girls was his girlfriend.

The boys from Money found it hard to believe Till. One of them said, "Hey, there's a *white* girl in that store there. I bet you won't go in there and talk to her." So Till went into the store to buy some candy, and on his way out, he said, "Bye, baby" to the white woman behind the counter.

Till wasn't from Mississippi. He really didn't know what he was doing.

After Till came out of the store, one of the boys went and told Curtis Jones what his young cousin had done. "Say, man," the boy told Jones, "you got a crazy cousin. He just went in there and said 'Bye' to that white woman."

And right then the old man who was playing checkers with Jones stood right up and told Till urgently, "Boy, y'all better get out of here. They're ready to come out of that there store and blow your brains out."

Jones and Till did not tell Mose Wright about the incident. Wright was Till's uncle, and Till was staying with him at the time. The boys hoped that everyone would forget about the incident.

Three days later, about 2:30 in the morning, two men came to Wright's front door. One man was Roy Bryant, whose wife had been the woman in the store. The other man was J. W. Milam, Bryant's brother-in-law.

According to Wright, who would later testify against Bryant and Milam at their trial, this is what happened:

> When I opened the door, there was a man standing with a pistol in one hand and a flashlight in the other hand. And he asked me did I have two boys there from Chicago. I told him, "I have." And he said, "I wants the boy that done all that talk."
>
> And they march him to the car, and they ask someone there, Was this the boy? And the answer was yes. And they drove toward Money.

The following Wednesday, Emmett Till was found at the bottom of the Tallahatchie River with a 70-pound cotton-gin fan tied around his neck. It was tied with barbed wire. He had been beaten and then shot through the head. His body was so mutilated that Mose Wright could identify him only by a ring that he wore with his initials carved into it.

Partly because he was so badly beaten, and partly because he was a northerner, Till's death captured the attention of the nation. At the funeral in Chicago, Till's mother insisted on an open casket so that "all the world can see what they did to my boy." Later, *Jet* magazine published a photo of Till's disfigured corpse. It was a photo that a generation of African Americans would not easily forget.

Because of Mose Wright's testimony, Bryant and Milam were brought to trial in Sumner, Mississippi, but no one really thought they would be convicted. As far as most white southerners were concerned, Till had got what he had coming.

Sheriff H. C. Strider of Tallahatchie County spoke for many when he said, "We never had any trouble until some of our southern niggers go up North, and the NAACP talks to them, and they come back home."

The idea that southern blacks were happy with their life on the plantation was one that made it much easier for southern whites to sleep at night. Of course it was far from the truth, but whites still clung to it. In their minds, if there was trouble, it had to be the work of outside troublemakers from the North.

By agreeing to testify against white men, Mose Wright was risking his life. But Wright's bravery did little to change the outcome of the trial. Despite the evidence and Wright's positive identification of Bryant and Milam, the two men were found not guilty by the all-white jury after less than an hour of deliberation. In his summation, one defense lawyer had told the jury that he was sure "every last Anglo-Saxon one of you has the courage to free these men." And he was right.

Among other things, the Till case showed that the NAACP's strategy of legal action had not and could not by itself solve all the problems that blacks faced. White racists in the South could still do pretty much as they pleased. After all, Bryant and Milam had killed Till. Everyone knew it. And they still walked away free men. The *Brown* decision hadn't changed that.

In Ruleville, meanwhile, Fannie Lou Hamer went about her life as usual. She spent long days picking cotton, and she devoted herself to her family. She continued to hope and pray for change, but she could do little else. After all, what could one woman do to change a great society?

IT BEGINS IN MONTGOMERY

> ❝ *The Emancipation Proclamation [which freed the slaves] was issued in 1863, ninety-odd years ago. I believe in gradualism. I also believe that ninety-odd years is pretty gradual.* ❞
>
> **THURGOOD MARSHALL of the NAACP Legal Defense Fund**

L ike Fannie Lou Hamer, a black woman in a society ruled by white men, Rosa Parks dreamed of a better life for African Americans. And also like Hamer, she had a powerful weapon: a burning desire to fight for the cause of justice.

On the night of December 1, 1955, after an exhausting day of work, Parks, a 42-year-old seamstress, boarded a bus for home. She worked at a downtown department store in Montgomery, Alabama. When she got on the bus, she took a seat in the back, immediately behind the front section reserved for whites.

At the next stop, six more whites got on the bus. Because there weren't enough seats for them up front, the bus driver, following Alabama law, expanded the white section. He ordered Parks and three other African Americans to get up and stand further in the back.

The others got up, as blacks did every day in Montgomery, but Parks refused. The bus driver called the police.

When the policeman arrived, he asked Parks, "Why don't you stand up?"

"I don't think I should have to stand up," Parks answered. "Why do you push us around?"

"I do not know," the policeman answered, "but the law is the law and you are under arrest."

Rosa Parks was not the first African American to refuse to give up her seat on a bus. A few months earlier, a 15-year-old African-American girl had been pulled off a bus, handcuffed, and jailed for refusing to give up her seat. But Parks wasn't just an ordinary seamstress. Besides possessing a forceful will, she had been secretary of the local chapter of the NAACP for a number of years.

Her boss at the NAACP, E. D. Nixon, came down to the jail to bail her out. He told her that he believed her case could be used to end segregation on Montgomery's city buses.

That night, Nixon and the Rev. Ralph Abernathy, of the First Baptist Church, called for a one-day boycott of the city buses. A protest meeting was also called for December 3, two days before the boycott.

Organizing Montgomery's 50,000 African Americans in just two days would normally have been an impossible task. But the city had a few determined groups of African-American activists who were equal to the task. Among these groups, the Women's Political Council played a particularly crucial role. One of its members, Jo Ann Robinson, stayed up all night printing 35,000 copies of the boycott notice on a hand-operated mimeograph machine.

At that time, in December 1955, Dr. Martin Luther King, Jr., had just taken over as pastor of Montgomery's Dexter Avenue Baptist Church. He was only 26 years old, and relatively unknown outside his own congregation. But the other ministers knew about him.

King was the son of a prominent Atlanta minister. He had attended Morehouse College, Pennsylvania's Crozer Theological Seminary (where he had been graduated first in his class), and Boston University, where he had received a Ph.D. degree in philosophy.

On the morning of December 5, the day of the boycott, King was up at 6 A.M. As he stood on his porch, he watched bus after bus go by. There was not one African-American rider on any of them. The 25,000 African Americans who normally rode the buses walked, taxied, bicycled, and even hitchhiked their way around Montgomery that day. But none of them took a bus. The boycott was a complete success.

It was so successful, in fact, that at a community meeting that night, it was decided to continue the boycott. The meeting that night was a turning point in the fight to desegregate Montgomery's buses. But it was more than that. It could even be argued that the modern civil rights movement was born that night. African-American protest had at last developed into a true mass movement. The entire community took part, not just a few NAACP lawyers.

That night, the Montgomery Improvement Association (MIA) was founded to direct the boycott. After Nixon turned down the job of running the MIA, the Rev. Martin Luther King, Jr., was elected its president. There were two reasons why King got the job. The first was that he had not been in town long enough "for the city fathers to put their hand on him," Nixon said. The other reason was that he was such an intelligent and eloquent speaker.

King gave the Montgomery boycott a new philosophy. In a few years' time, this would become the philosophy of the whole civil rights movement. King's ideas were based on those of Mohandas K. Gandhi, leader of India's struggle for independence from Great Britain, and the American writer Henry David Thoreau. King shared their belief in the principle of nonviolent "civil disobedience." That meant peacefully disobeying laws that were felt to be illegal or immoral. It also meant never responding to violence with more violence.

King felt that civil disobedience fit the African-American situation because Alabama's state segregation codes broke federal laws as well as moral ones. This gave King a legal basis for his protests, because under Article VI of the U.S. Constitution, federal law supersedes, or overrules, state law. It was an issue that NAACP lawyers had already settled in court many times before.

As a minister and a leader, however, King was more interested in moral laws than in government ones. The fight, King declared, was not against whites but against injustice. The most important weapon, he said, was love. King was arrested and threatened, his house was bombed, but still he refused the armed guards that were offered to protect him. He would not hate, he said.

All during this time, Fannie Lou Hamer continued to pick cotton in Ruleville, for the most part unaware of what was happening elsewhere in the South. But she came to the same conclusion about hate. Even after she was beaten in Winona, Hamer said, "It wouldn't solve any problem for me to hate whites just because they hate me. Oh, there's so much hate, only God has kept the Negro sane."

Under King's inspired leadership, the Montgomery boycott was close to 100-percent effective. It hurt both the bus companies and the downtown stores. But it was still uncertain whether that would be enough to end bus-seat segregation.

As the boycott stretched on into 1956, the whites who ran the city began to fight back. In January, Mayor W. A. Gayle announced a new get-tough policy. King was arrested for driving at 30 miles per hour in a 25-miles-per-hour zone. Other African-American leaders were soon arrested on similarly trivial charges.

When these arrests failed to stop the boycotters, King and more than 100 other MIA leaders were charged with breaking an antiboycott law that was so old no one besides the mayor even remembered it existed. The city also began lifting the licenses of African-American car-pool drivers and pressuring insurance companies to cancel African Americans' policies.

To keep the boycott going while it was under attack, Fred Gray, a civil rights lawyer, filed suit in federal court, claiming that bus segregation violated the 14th Amendment. On June 4, 1956, a federal district court agreed with him and declared the bus laws unconstitutional. The city appealed, but on November 13, the U.S. Supreme Court upheld the decision and abolished segregation in public transportation.

Negotiations with the city followed. Finally, on December 21, 1956, King and other MIA leaders ended the 382-day boycott. They boarded a bus of the Montgomery City Lines, and they sat in the front seats.

In the end, it was legal action in the courts that brought final victory. But the Montgomery boycott proved to African Americans everywhere that they could change the laws by direct action.

Before Montgomery, the gradualist—slow but steady—approach of the NAACP had prevailed, as had white liberal leadership. But after Montgomery, African Americans themselves began to take over the leadership of the civil rights movement. They had waited long enough.

"The Emancipation Proclamation [which freed the slaves] was issued in 1863, ninety-odd years ago," Thurgood Marshall said at the time. "I believe in gradualism. I also believe that ninety-odd years is pretty gradual."

THE SIGNS OF THE TIMES

The Montgomery boycott sparked black America into action as the old approach of gradualism died out overnight. Inspired by the success of the boycott, African Americans throughout the South began organizing protests of their own. Many of these protests focused on public school systems.

In Little Rock, Arkansas, for example, there was a well-publicized school integration fight in the fall of 1957. Acting against a federal court order, Governor Orval Faubus had called out the Arkansas National Guard to block nine black students

The Little Rock Nine are escorted into Central High School by U.S. troops sent to protect them.

from attending all-white Central High.

Like most presidents, Dwight D. Eisenhower preferred to work quietly behind the scenes. But Faubus had gone too far in blocking desegregation. Eisenhower was forced to send in federal troops to make sure that the court order was obeyed.

Little Rock was a sign of things to come. It was the first time a state government had directly challenged federal authority in a civil rights matter. But it would certainly not be the last.

Also in 1957, Congress passed a new civil rights law, the first since Reconstruction. The Civil Rights Act of 1957 came about in response to the Montgomery bus boycott. It wasn't very effective, though. Its only lasting consequence was the creation of a civil rights division in the Justice Department.

So, willing no more to rely on the government, the civil rights movement forged ahead.

The next major showdown occurred in Greensboro, North

Carolina, in February 1960. The Woolworth's store in downtown Greensboro was much like any other Woolworth's store in the country. It was even like Woolworth's stores are now. It sold shampoo and pencils and scissors and rubber bands, and it had a lunch counter. In 1960, though, African Americans weren't allowed to eat at Woolworth's lunch counters in the South.

On the afternoon of February 1, 1960, four African-American students from North Carolina Agricultural and Technical College entered the downtown Greensboro Woolworth's and sat down at its lunch counter. The names of the students were Ezell Blair, Jr., David Richmond, Franklin McCain, and Joseph McNeil. They were all freshmen, and they were all well-dressed and polite young men. They each ordered nothing more than a cup of coffee.

None of them was served. Instead, they were insulted and roughed up by some of the whites eating lunch at the counter. Remembering their nonviolent principles, however, the four students accepted the abuse and remained in their seats until closing time.

The next day they were back again, but this time with 16 more students and a few reporters from national wire services. The third day, they came back again with even more students, 50 this time, and some of them were white.

None of the African-American students was served any coffee. But in the meantime, the reporters let the rest of the country know what they were doing, and that made all the difference.

Two years earlier, in 1958, a black teacher in Oklahoma City named Clara Luper had led a series of lunch counter sit-ins. These sit-ins, however, were reported only by the local newspapers and television stations. As a result, they spread no further than Wichita, Kansas.

It wasn't until Greensboro that the sit-in movement received national attention. And once it did, it exploded. By April 1960, sit-ins had spread to 77 other cities. Within the year, there were an estimated 50,000 to 75,000 young people actively involved. At least 3,600 of these were arrested and went to jail, many for months.

The sit-ins were widely considered to be great victories for the movement. There were many reasons why. Media coverage of the sit-ins, for instance, helped make the American public more aware of the discrimination faced by African Americans. Also, the sit-ins spawned boycotts of chain stores that practiced segregation. These nationwide boycotts hurt the chain stores' sales and caused them to rethink their segregationist policies.

But the greatest contribution of the sit-ins was the generation of young African-American leaders it brought into the movement. For many African Americans, the sit-ins were their first taste of organized political activity. For example, Robert Moses, James Forman, and John Lewis of the Student Nonviolent Coordinating Committee (SNCC) all got their starts in political activity during the sit-ins.

Thus from Montgomery to Greensboro, the idea of direct action was catching on. College students, who were neither old enough nor poor enough to be scared, joined the movement. While the NAACP may have been overly cautious in the past, its Legal Defense Fund now contributed generously to the students' bail. It also helped them resolve the many legal problems they encountered.

The sit-in movement was so successful that by the spring of 1961, the demonstrations and boycotts had almost completely ended restaurant segregation. Now the new young leaders looked elsewhere for instances of discrimination that they could challenge. The battleground they chose next was interstate travel.

Because segregation itself had not yet been outlawed by the federal government, many state laws segregating local buses and bus stations were still considered legal. Interstate travel, however, was a special case. It was a business activity that crossed state lines. Therefore, according to the Constitution, Congress

At this Woolworth's lunch counter in Greensboro, North Carolina, the sit-in movement started.

had the power to regulate it. Citing this interstate commerce clause of the Constitution, the Supreme Court ruled in the case of *Boynton v. Virginia* (1960) that segregation in interstate travel was illegal.

The next step was to make the federal government enforce the *Boynton* decision. One way to force federal action was to create a situation in which state laws would be broken while federal laws were being observed.

On May 4, 1961, 13 people boarded a Greyhound bus in Washington, D.C., and set out for the Deep South. The group was organized by the Congress of Racial Equality (CORE). It was made up of seven blacks and six whites. They were called the Freedom Riders.

The Freedom Riders planned to travel through the most segregated parts of the South and openly break the state segregation laws that the Supreme Court had declared illegal.

Among the riders were John Lewis of SNCC, who had already been arrested five times before at various sit-ins, and James Farmer, the national director of CORE. Joining them were James Peck, a white CORE staff member who had been jailed during World War II for being a pacifist, and Walter Bergman, a retired school administrator, and his wife. Both Mr. and Mrs. Bergman were over 60 years old.

Each of the Freedom Riders was committed to nonviolence, but many southern whites were not. The first attack came in a white bus stop waiting room at Rock Hill, South Carolina, where two Freedom Riders were beaten. But that was nothing compared to what happened on May 14 in Anniston, Alabama.

At the Anniston station, a mob attacked the bus with chains and iron rods, breaking the windows and slashing the tires. The bus managed to travel a few miles out of Anniston, but part of the mob followed in cars. When the bus had to stop because of the flat tires, the crowd that had followed it set the bus on fire, destroying it completely.

As the Freedom Riders tried to escape, one African-American rider was hit with a brutal blow to the head. Twelve others had to be hospitalized for smoke poisoning.

But the Freedom Rides went on, and so did the beatings. The next attack came on a Trailways bus when eight white men got on and began pulling black riders out of the bus's front seats. When Peck and Bergman came forward to help, they were beaten as well.

Later, as this same bus pulled into Birmingham, Alabama, another mob attacked the riders, beating them and sending Peck to the hospital with severe cuts on his face. The Birmingham police did nothing to stop the beatings.

Despite the violence and the injuries, John Lewis and SNCC refused to back down. Lewis flew to Nashville and organized a new group of African-American students to take the place of the injured riders.

A bus carrying Freedom Riders is firebombed outside Birmingham.

Bus companies did not want to carry the Nashville volunteers, but on May 20, Lewis finally found a bus that would take them to Montgomery. Governor John Patterson of Alabama had claimed he would protect them, but when they arrived in Montgomery, they were met at the station by a howling gang of 300 angry whites. There were no police in sight.

It was the worst riot yet. Lewis himself was clubbed to the ground by men with baseball bats. One black student lay unconscious on the floor for 20 minutes because no white ambulance would take him to a hospital. Even John Seigenthaler of the Justice Department, President Kennedy's personal representative, was beaten unconscious while attempting to protect a Freedom Rider on the street.

The Associated Press reported that it took 20 minutes for the police to arrive. In that time, the crowd had swelled to such a size—a thousand or more—that it took the police more than two hours to break it up.

Little of this activity reached small Ruleville, however, where there were no Freedom Rides. Washington and Little Rock were both very far away. Even the news had trouble getting through. "Livin' in the country," Hamer said, "[even] if you had a little radio, by the time you got in at night, you'd be too tired to listen at what was goin' on."

Mostly, time just passed. In the spring, the cotton was planted. In the fall, it was picked. In the world of the sharecropper, nothing seemed to change but the seasons.

Then, on Sunday, August 26, 1962, something did change. Fannie Lou Hamer attended her weekly church service that day. After the service was over, the minister announced that there would be a mass meeting at the church the following night. The meeting was co-sponsored by SNCC and the Southern Christian Leadership Conference (SCLC).

Not many people in the town knew what a mass meeting was, or what it would be about. It was the first one ever held in Ruleville. But because it was held at the church, people took it seriously. Just as in Montgomery, churches in rural Mississippi played a crucial role in organizing the African-American community.

Charles McLaurin was a SNCC volunteer at the time. He remembered those early days of organizing the people of Ruleville:

> In the summer of 1962 I [worked] in Ruleville setting up voter registration drives. We started by knocking on doors, trying to get people to go and register at the courthouse in Indianola, which was 26 miles away.
>
> After about a week of knocking on doors, we had only gotten about six people to try and register, so we decided to have a big mass rally to stimulate some interest in the community. We had the rally and people from the plantations around Ruleville came.

When Fannie Lou Hamer heard about the meeting, she asked

her husband, Pap, if they could go. "And he said if we picked enough cotton that day then he would bring us that night. So we worked hard so we could come to the mass meeting," Hamer recalled.

August nights in Mississippi can be very hot and muggy. It can be very uncomfortable to sit indoors in a small, closed space like the Ruleville church, especially when it's filled with people. But that Monday night it didn't matter. Nothing else seemed to matter, because everyone at the mass meeting was paying very close attention.

The meeting was run by two very important, and very different, organizations. The SCLC had been founded in 1957 by a group of African-American ministers, led by Martin Luther King, Jr. The SCLC's job was to coordinate the civil rights activities of ministers throughout the South. It was an organization of organizations, not one that people could join.

The second group, SNCC, had been organized two years later, in 1960, at a conference called by King and Ella Baker, then acting executive director of the SCLC. SNCC was formed to take advantage of the energies of students and other young people. It was an organization that people could and did join. Within a few years, in fact, SNCC would become the most active, and least patient, arm of the civil rights movement. (The abbreviation SNCC is pronounced "snick.")

The two key speakers at the meeting were James Bevel, the SCLC field secretary for Mississippi, and James Forman, SNCC's executive secretary. Like the SCLC, Bevel believed in moderate, cautious change. Forman, on the other hand, was a man of more radical temperament. They represented two different approaches that the movement could take.

That night in Ruleville, though, both Bevel and Forman could agree on one thing: If anything was ever going to change in Mississippi, Fannie Lou Hamer and her neighbors would have to register to vote.

This is how Hamer remembered the meeting:

James Bevel preached that night. With a lot of people, you can get them involved around sermons. So he preached that night from the 16th chapter of Matthew, the third verse, "Discerning the Signs of the Times."

He talked about how a man could look out and see a cloud and predict it's going to rain, and it would become so; but still he couldn't tell what was happening right around him. . . .

Then Jim Forman talked about how it was our constitutional right to register and to vote. Until then . . . I didn't know a Negro could register and vote.

Hamer and her neighbors heard the words and were moved to action.

"When they asked for those to raise their hands who'd go down to the courthouse [and register]," Hamer later recalled, "I raised mine. I guess if I'd had any sense I'd a been a little scared, but what was the point of being scared? The only thing they could do to me was kill me, and it seemed like they'd been trying to do that a little bit at a time ever since I could remember."

Z GOING TO REGISTER

❝ Everybody on the bus was shaking with fear... [but] then this voice singing church songs just came out of the crowd and began to calm everybody.... It was then that I learned that Fannie Lou Hamer was on the bus. Somebody said, 'That's Fannie Lou, she know how to sing.' ❞

CHARLES MCLAURIN, member of the Student Nonviolent Coordinating Committee (SNCC)

When the Ruleville mass meeting ended that night, SNCC worker Robert Moses helped make arrangements for the trip to Indianola, where the circuit clerk had his office. The 18 volunteers who had raised their hands agreed to travel the following Friday.

Hamer may not have known it at the time, but Moses would become not only her greatest influence, but also one of the most important African-American leaders in Mississippi.

Robert Moses was born in Harlem. As a boy, he attended Stuyvesant High School in Manhattan, a public school in New

York City for very bright students. After Stuyvesant, he went to Hamilton College in upstate New York, where he majored in philosophy.

From there, Moses went on to Harvard University, where he received a master's degree in 1957. For a few years he taught mathematics at Horace Mann, a prominent private school in New York City.

Then in 1960, the passion of the sit-in movement and the cause of civil rights drew him to the South. Moses knew that integrated bus terminals and lunch counters were an important first step. But he also knew that there was only one way for African Americans to achieve real power. They had to vote. Black voting was something the white segregationists simply could not tolerate. But this was exactly what Moses was determined to achieve.

If African Americans could organize and vote, Moses reasoned, they could abolish the Jim Crow laws themselves, without having to resort to the courts. By controlling the sheriff's office, for instance, they could make sure racist beatings and murders did not go unpunished.

This is why much of the most serious violence of the civil rights years was linked to the right to vote. In Miami, Florida, an African-American man who had led a registration drive was killed when a bomb blew apart his house on Christmas Eve. In Mississippi in 1955, an African-American minister and three others were shot to death when they tried to register to vote. There were no convictions in either case.

In 1960, Congress passed a civil rights act that created somewhat tougher laws against racial intimidation. The Civil Rights Act of 1960 gave the courts more power to help enforce voting rights. For the first time, voting registrars had to preserve registration records and account to the federal government for their actions.

In August 1961, just one year before Fannie Lou Hamer decided she would try to register, Robert Moses himself was badly beaten. He had been trying to help two African Americans register to vote in Amite County, Mississippi, down near the Louisiana border. He was beaten right inside the courthouse, by the sheriff's cousin.

When Fannie Lou Hamer boarded that bus for Indianola on Friday, August 31, 1962, she didn't know all of this, but she knew enough. It was impossible to grow up in Mississippi and not know what angry whites might do whenever blacks tried to organize.

Hamer, however, was not to be denied. This was the chance she had been waiting for all her life. She felt a passion to vote, not unlike the passion she felt in church or the passion she felt singing. It wasn't because of politics that she desperately wanted to vote; it was because of morality. Justice had inspired her.

Moses had arranged for an African-American man from nearby Bolivar County to drive the group from Ruleville to the county courthouse in Indianola, 26 miles away. The man owned an old yellow school bus that he used in the summer to carry plantation workers to the fields and in the winter to take poor migrant workers down to Florida, where they could usually find work in the orange groves.

When the bus arrived in Indianola that day, the eighteen who had come to register filed into the office. But the circuit clerk, a man named Cecil B. Campbell, sent all but two of them out again, telling them that they could only come in two at a time. Though the group had elected no leader, Hamer was one of the two who stayed inside.

To register to vote in Mississippi at that time there was a literacy test. Each would-be voter had to write the answers to 22 questions. Of these, 21 called for simple information: name, address, job, and so on. The last question was the tricky one. It required the applicant to explain one of the 286 sections of the Mississippi state constitution.

The first part of the test was easy for anyone who could read and write. Sometimes registrars would even help illiterate blacks with this part. That was because the whites in power wanted to know this kind of information about blacks who were trying to register to vote. They wanted to know the names of these blacks, where they lived, and where they worked in case any whites decided to take action against them later.

In 1954, segregationist whites in Mississippi had formed local chapters of an organization called the Citizens' Council, or sometimes the White Citizens' Council. Made up of politicians, bankers, lawyers, and businessmen, the Citizens' Council had only one purpose: to enforce the Jim Crow laws by whatever means were necessary.

In many cases the registrars were themselves members. Often they would turn information from African-American voting forms over to the Citizens' Councils or the Ku Klux Klan. The Klan's response was usually violent, while the Citizens' Council used economic power. Blacks who tried to register were usually fired from their jobs. Whites who tried to help them were either denied loans and or had banks foreclose on their mortgages.

The last part of the test, though, the part about explaining a section of the Mississippi constitution, was nearly impossible for a black to pass. It didn't matter that most poor blacks had no idea Mississippi even had a constitution. It didn't even matter that some registrars could hardly read themselves.

What did matter was that the blacks who took the test had to explain the meaning of the section to the satisfaction of the registrar, who was always white. Whenever the applicant was black, the registrar was almost never satisfied.

Fannie Lou Hamer remembered:

> That literacy test was rough. The registrar, Mr. Campbell, brought this big black book over there, and pointed out something for me to read. It was the 16th section of the Constitution of Mississippi . . . dealing with *de facto* laws.
>
> I knowed as much about a *de facto* law as a horse knows about Christmas Day. And he told me to read it and copy.

Then after I had copied it, give a reasonable interpretation. So you know about what happened to me. Well, I flunked the test, you know, 'cause I didn't know what in the world was a *de facto* law. Still don't really know what it is.

It took the whole day for the 18 applicants from Ruleville to take the test, two at a time. In the end, they all flunked it. And at four-thirty in the afternoon, they all got back on the bus and headed home. They were all very tired. It had been a long day.

A few miles outside of Indianola, their bus was stopped by some state police, and everyone was ordered to get out. Led by Hamer, they all started singing "Have a Little Talk with Jesus." Then the police ordered them back on the bus and told the driver to follow the police car back to Indianola.

Back in Indianola, both Robert Moses, who had returned to Ruleville to accompany the group that day, and the bus driver were arrested. They were fined $100 because the bus was too yellow and might be mistaken for a real school bus.

"Now ain't that ridiculous?" Fannie Lou Hamer said. Hamer and the other riders knew, of course, that the police were simply harassing them. She said:

> This same bus had been used year after year...and he [the driver] had never been arrested before. But the day he tried...to carry us to Indianola, they fined him a hundred dollars.
>
> [Then] when they started to carry him to jail, we all was going to jail with him 'cause we didn't know what it was all about. But we knowed we should stick with him because he carried us down there.
>
> So then the [police] made us stop, and they finally cut his fine down to $30, and all of us together—not one, but all of us together—had enough to pay his fine.

THE BATTLE FOR MISSISSIPPI

No school in our state will be integrated while I am your governor.

ROSS BARNETT,
Governor of Mississippi

When Fannie Lou Hamer finally got back home to the plantation that evening, bad news was waiting for her. Her daughter and one of Pap's cousins told her that the plantation boss, Mr. Marlowe, had been "raising a lot of Cain."

Fannie Lou Hamer had worked on the Marlowe plantation for 18 years. She had cared for Marlowe's children, cleaned his house, nursed his family, and even baked and sent cakes to him while he was overseas during the war. And all of that was in addition to her regular duties as a timekeeper on the plantation.

When she came back from trying to register to vote, though,

everything had instantly changed. When Pap Hamer returned from the fields that night, he told Fannie Lou that Marlowe was very angry because he had been told of her trip to Indianola to register. Marlowe was probably told by a member of the local Citizens' Council, which must have received a call from the registrar's office.

Soon Marlowe himself appeared at the Hamers' house.

"Is Fannie Lou in the house?" he asked Pap Hamer.

"Yes, sir, she is in the house," Pap said.

"So, did you tell her what I said?"

"Yes, sir."

"I mean that she's got to go back and withdraw her registration or she'll have to leave?"

At that point, Fannie Lou, who had been inside the house listening, got up and walked out.

"Did Pap tell you what I said?" Marlowe asked her.

"Yes, sir, he did," she replied.

"Well, you're going to have to tell me whether you're going back to withdraw your registration or you're going to leave here. We're not ready for this in Mississippi."

"Mr. Marlowe," Fannie Lou Hamer said, "I didn't go to Indianola to register for you. I went down there to register for myself."

"We are not going to have this in Mississippi," said Marlowe, "and you will have to withdraw. I am looking for your answer, yea or nay?"

Fannie Lou Hamer just looked at him.

"I will give you until tomorrow morning," Marlowe said finally.

But Fannie Lou wouldn't be seeing Marlowe in the morning. She left that same night. "I knowed I wasn't goin' back to withdraw," she said.

Pap Hamer had been ordered not to leave the plantation while the harvest was underway, but he drove Fannie Lou the four and a half miles into town anyway. They had some friends on Byron Street, the Tuckers, who took her in.

Pap and the rest of the family had to stay on the plantation, though. Pap had been warned that if he left with Fannie Lou, he would lose the job he had held for the last 30 years and all the family's furniture would be taken away.

So Pap Hamer stayed on with Dorothy and Virgie Ree, but he was nervous. He had seen some buckshot shells in the plantation's maintenance shed. That was unusual because it wasn't hunting season yet.

It turned out Pap was right to be worried. On the night of September 10, 1962, ten days after Fannie Lou moved in with the Tuckers, a band of white men with guns made a late-night ride through town.

Sixteen shots were fired into the Tuckers' home. The McDonald house, where Student Nonviolent Coordinating Committee (SNCC) volunteers were staying, was also hit. But the real hardship came at the Herman Sissel house, where two women students from Jackson State College were hit, one receiving a buckshot wound in the head.

In one way or another, each of these targets was associated with SNCC's voter registration drive.

"All they had done was try to register, or carry somebody to try to register," Hamer said. "And this is the kind of pressure we went through."

That night, Fannie Lou Hamer fled Ruleville, fearing for her life. She traveled secretly to her niece's house in Cascilla, a town in neighboring Tallahatchie County, about 40 miles from Ruleville.

Charles McLaurin remembered:

> After [the shootings], Hamer moved out into Tallahatchie County, and I didn't see her again for about two weeks.
>
> Then word came from Bob Moses to go and find Mrs. Hamer and bring her to the annual SNCC conference in Nashville.
>
> So I searched all day getting a little lead here and a little

lead there on through the county. Finally the last directions I got were to go to Cascilla. They said you'll find her at a little brown house sitting up on a hill.

That evening it was raining like hell. Thundering and lightning and raining, and I was out there searching. I finally saw this little house with smoke coming out of the chimney. I knocked on the door and a voice told me to come in. And there was a lady in a chair with her back to me putting wood into a big pot-bellied stove. I said, "I'm looking for Fannie Lou Hamer." This was my first real meeting with her.

I told her that Bob Moses and the people at SNCC asked me to pick her up and take her on to the Nashville conference. And she got right up and went to getting her stuff. I'd never met her, and she didn't know me. She couldn't have known whether I was kidnapping her or what. But she just got right up and came.

In the meantime, things were heating up elsewhere in Mississippi that fall of 1962, particularly in Oxford to the north. Oxford is the home of the University of Mississippi, also known as Ole Miss. James Meredith was at that time fighting to become its first African-American student.

With its magnolias and its honeysuckle, its classic Greek architecture, and its broad and gracious lawns, Ole Miss was the pride of the state. In fact, throughout the South, Ole Miss was cherished as a symbol of the one-time glory of the Confederacy. At that time, it was one of the least likely places one would expect to find a black face, except perhaps among the cafeteria or janitorial staffs.

Meredith first sued for admission to Ole Miss in the summer of 1961. It happened that he filed suit in federal district court in Jackson at the same time that the Freedom Riders were themselves converging on the city.

Meredith's lawyers were familiar figures in the federal courtrooms of the South: Jack Greenberg and Constance Baker

Motley of the National Association for the Advancement of Colored People (NAACP) Legal Defense Fund.

James Meredith was born on a farm in Attala County in the center of Mississippi. As a boy, he walked to school and back eight miles each day. After school, he would help his father on the farm, or sometimes he would catch crickets and grasshoppers and sell them to white fishermen.

Meredith's father, Moses "Cap" Meredith, never had any schooling past the fourth grade, but he was determined that his ten children would do better. And they did, all of them graduating from high school and seven of them going on to college.

After high school, though, James Meredith temporarily passed up college for the air force, where he served for eight years. During that time, Meredith also got married and fathered a son. He received an honorable discharge.

After leaving the air force, Meredith enrolled first at the all-black Jackson State. But he quickly realized that the courses at Jackson State were inadequate, so he applied for a transfer to Ole Miss.

Meredith often appeared to be quiet and shy. But given the task he had set for himself, he would have to be tough. The federal courts might force the university to register him, but it was up to Meredith himself to deal with the threats and abuse from his fellow students. Once he started down the road to Oxford, there was no turning back without disastrous results for both himself and the movement.

Meredith wanted to begin classes in the fall of 1961, but his court battle stretched on and on for over a year. One of his closest friends during that time was Medgar Evers, head of the Mississippi NAACP. Evers had once tried to integrate Ole Miss himself, but had failed. Now he worked hard to see that Meredith did not.

From the beginning, it was clear that the federal district judge hearing the case would not be sympathetic. Despite the fact that everyone in Mississippi knew otherwise, the state argued that there was no policy of segregation at Ole Miss. Somehow, the judge agreed. When his decision was handed down, though, the U.S. Court of Appeals for the Fifth Circuit immediately reversed it. The court of appeals ordered that Meredith be admitted to the university.

Before the court of appeals would make its order final, however, it wanted an answer to this question: Who would enforce the order?

With Little Rock still fresh in their minds, the nine appeals court judges met privately with President Kennedy's representative, Assistant Attorney General Burke Marshall. The full court put the question to Marshall directly: Was the president prepared to enforce the order directing Meredith to be admitted to the University of Mississippi?

Marshall said that the president was prepared to use whatever force was necessary to enforce the court's order. But he also told the judges that President Kennedy preferred a political solution, if one could be arranged. The president was already thinking about a second term. He did not want to lose any support among southern whites.

That Kennedy preferred a gradual approach was nothing new to the leaders of the movement. They knew that presidents rarely stuck their necks out for black civil rights. But they also knew that Kennedy would have to act if the pressure of events left him no other choice.

The position of the state of Mississippi was simple. Court order or no court order, no black student would ever be admitted to Ole Miss under any circumstances. "No school in our state will be integrated while I am your governor," Governor Ross Barnett had said.

A man of his word, Governor Barnett flew up to the Ole Miss campus in Oxford on September 20, 1962, to defy the federal court order and turn James Meredith away. Five days later, when Meredith tried to register again at the university's Jackson office, Barnett was there, too, once again personally blocking the way.

It was at this time that Kennedy decided he would have to

move against Barnett, much as Eisenhower finally moved against Governor Faubus in the Little Rock crisis.

The president ordered to Oxford 400 federal marshals under Deputy Attorney General Nicholas Katzenbach. The marshals arrived on campus on Sunday, September 30. Their plan was to secure the campus, bring Meredith in that night, and then register him first thing Monday morning.

There were a few things the president hadn't counted on, though. For one, whites from all over the South had come to Oxford to stop Meredith. For another, it was squirrel-hunting season, and almost every pickup truck had a few guns mounted behind the cab. This was a dangerous combination.

At first things went smoothly. That Sunday, the campus was

Determined to register, James Meredith arrives at Ole Miss escorted by U.S. marshals and reporters.

practically deserted because most of the students had gone to Jackson for the football game against Kentucky. When the students began returning Sunday night, however, they saw the federal marshals, and quickly tempers flared.

President Kennedy announced that he would speak to the citizens of Mississippi that night. But at 8:00 P.M., just as Kennedy went on the air, a riot exploded on the campus of Ole Miss. There were bursts of gunfire. Students threw firebombs made from Coca-Cola bottles at the campus building that was serving as Katzenbach's headquarters. The federal marshals were allowed to use tear gas only to control the crowd, and that wasn't nearly enough.

As the riot got further out of hand, Katzenbach called in the army to restore order. Nearly 30,000 federal troops rolled in. By morning the campus was quiet, but the damage had been done. Over 160 marshals had been injured, 28 of them shot, and 2 bystanders were dead.

In a speech that few on the campus heard, President Kennedy said, "Americans are free . . . to disagree with the law, but not to disobey it." In Oxford that night, he proved his point, but at great expense.

"Of course the President's going to win in the end," said Burke Marshall. "He's got the whole Armed Forces of the United States. He can call in the Air Force. He can bring Navy ships up the Mississippi River. He can call out the Army, as he did. He can drop parachuters in. I suppose he could shoot missiles at Oxford, Mississippi. So he's going to win at the end."

Monday morning, James Meredith was enrolled as the first African-American student at the University of Mississippi.

And just as Meredith had toughed it out, Fannie Lou Hamer was determined to do the same. After the Nashville conference, she decided to return to Ruleville despite the danger.

Back in Ruleville, though, things were even worse than when she had left, if that was possible. Pap had been fired from his job. The family had lost its car, its furniture, and its house.

A friend of the Hamers was able to find them a place to stay in Ruleville, but the house had no running water. Even so, they could barely afford it because they couldn't find work. Nobody would hire Fannie Lou because of her registration activities. No one would hire Pap because he was Fannie Lou's husband and he had stood by her.

So what did Fannie Lou Hamer do, considering that trying to register to vote had caused all of her problems in the first place? On December 4, she went down to Indianola and tried to register again.

"You'll see me every thirty days until I pass," Hamer told the registrar.

WORKING FOR SNCC

> *" There was nothing they could do to me. They couldn't fire me, because I didn't have a job. They couldn't put me out of my house, because I didn't have one. There was nothing they could take from me any longer. "*

FANNIE LOU HAMER

The Student Nonviolent Coordinating Committee (SNCC) wasn't like most other civil rights organizations. Because it followed a legal strategy, the National Association for the Advancement of Colored People (NAACP) rarely sent people into small, backwater towns like Ruleville. But SNCC came to Ruleville because SNCC went everywhere in the rural South.

Led by young staff members and volunteers, SNCC favored forceful, direct action. Grass-roots organizing was its specialty.

In its first few years of existence, SNCC had focused its

attention on the sit-ins and the other mass demonstrations. But by the summer of 1961, some SNCC staff members, particularly Robert Moses, wanted to shift SNCC resources to voter-registration drives.

Moses admitted that the sit-ins had achieved some real gains. But he pointed out that the freedom to eat at a Woolworth's lunch counter was not the same as freedom from police brutality or the right to obtain a fair trial.

To win these civil rights in Mississippi, Moses argued, African Americans would have to influence the sheriffs and judges of Mississippi. And the only sure way to do that, he knew, was to register and vote. The system had to be changed at its roots.

In August 1961, SNCC decided to pursue both sit-ins and registration drives. Moses was picked to lead the registration effort.

Moses was the perfect man for this difficult job. He was already well known within the movement as a tireless and capable worker. And he was also a born leader. With large, tranquil eyes hidden behind thick, plastic-framed glasses, he spoke with a calm voice and chose his words slowly and carefully.

Perhaps Moses' style came from the time he spent as a mathematics teacher, but wherever it came from, it inspired and reassured the people with whom he worked. "He could walk into a place where a lynch mob had just left and make up a bed and prepare to go to sleep, as if the situation was normal," one SNCC worker said.

Moses set up SNCC field offices all over the state of Mississippi because the only way he saw to register African Americans to vote was to go out into the fields and talk to those who weren't registered.

Many of the unregistered African Americans would need help, of course. Like Fannie Lou Hamer herself, many didn't even know they could vote. Others would need help with the forms. Almost all of them would need help to pass the tricky literacy test.

But, as Moses knew, all of this could be taught. What would be more difficult to provide would be the courage each new registrant needed to challenge Mississippi's system of white domination. All their lives, the poor blacks of Mississippi had lived in fear of whites. All their lives, they had been told that whites were superior. Fannie Lou Hamer had never believed it, but she was one of the exceptions.

Most of Hamer's neighbors found it very difficult to forget what the whites had taught them, particularly when so many violent whites were happy to remind them of these lessons.

Fannie Lou Hamer returned to Ruleville that winter of 1962 as a field secretary for SNCC. She immediately started organizing a local poverty program. This included asking the federal government for food and clothing for the needy families of Ruleville. She also began the work of organizing the townspeople politically. This was her most important task. In the fields by day and in the churches by night, Hamer talked to people about the movement and about their right to vote.

In addition to all this, Hamer even found time to cook for all the SNCC workers who regularly came to town.

Fannie Lou Hamer soon became one of SNCC's most effective fundraisers. She often traveled north to speak to white audiences about the desperation of black Mississippians and their desire for change. "I'm sick and tired of being sick and tired," Hamer would tell them.

So far there had been no repeat of the September 10 shootings, but the harassment continued. One morning before daylight, two policemen came into the Hamers' bedroom with their guns drawn. They pretended to conduct a search, but they had no warrant. Their real purpose was to scare the Hamers.

Another time, the Hamers received a water bill for $9,000, when they didn't even have running water. Nevertheless, Pap was arrested over this bill.

These years were very difficult ones for the Hamers, though it must have helped to know that they had the movement behind them. Fannie Lou's $10-a-week SNCC salary barely allowed the family to get by, but friends and neighbors helped out when they could.

Still, it was difficult to keep going. After all, most SNCC volunteers were much younger and much better educated than Fannie Lou Hamer was. They also didn't have families to support. But what Fannie Lou Hamer lacked in those areas, she more than made up for in courage and determination.

January 10, 1963, was a Thursday. It was also the day that Fannie Lou Hamer, on her third try, became one of the first of Sunflower County's 30,000 African Americans to register to vote. She had been studying sections of the Mississippi state constitution, hoping to get one on the test that she could interpret. She did get one, and she passed.

When election day came that fall, however, Hamer was still denied her right to vote because she couldn't afford the money to pay the Mississippi poll tax.

THE WINONA JAIL

> **❝ The next thing I knew I was on the floor and they were all beating me with sticks and kicking me. One pulled me up and...another came behind me and started choking me with a billy stick. By this time my eye was all messed up, and my head was knocked open, and I was just screaming and trying to protect myself some way. ❞**
>
> JUNE JOHNSON, on her beating at age 14 in the Winona jail

In 1963, Winona, Mississippi, was a small town, even by southern standards. Only about six thousand people lived there. But because it was located right at the intersection of Mississippi's two major highways—Interstate 55 and State Route 82—it got a lot of traffic.

Much of this was interstate bus traffic. For example, the bus from Memphis, Tennessee, to the Mississippi state capital, Jackson, passed through Winona. So did the bus from Charleston, South Carolina, to Ruleville.

Fannie Lou Hamer left Mississippi with a few other Student Nonviolent Coordinating Committee (SNCC) workers on June 3, 1963, to attend a voter registration workshop in Charleston. The workshop lasted until June 8, when her group boarded a Continental Trailways bus for the return trip to Ruleville. On the morning of June 9, sometime between 10:30 and 11:00 A.M., the bus made a scheduled stop in Winona. From there, the group would head west toward Greenwood and Indianola.

Winona was familiar to Hamer because it was the seat of Montgomery County, where she had been born. In the summer of 1963, Winona was still strictly segregationist. This was not unusual for a town in the Mississippi Delta, that area of farmland made rich by the waters of the Mississippi River. What made Winona different, though, was that its bus terminal still separated the races into black and white.

Segregation in interstate travel had been banned since the fall of 1961. That was when the Interstate Commerce Commission (ICC), pressured by the Freedom Rides, had issued clear-cut rules against segregation in interstate bus facilities. (The ICC is the agency of the federal government that oversees interstate business.)

Because it serviced buses traveling between states, the Winona bus station was covered by these rules. But the station management ignored them and got away with it. The Kennedy administration could not be everywhere, nor did it wish to be.

Arriving in Winona after traveling all night, four of the SNCC workers got off the bus to get something to eat at the terminal. Two others went to use the washroom. Hamer, however, stayed on the bus until she saw all six of them come running out. Then she got off to see what was happening. One of her companions, Annelle Ponder, told her that the chief of police had ordered them out of the terminal. "Well, this is Mississippi for you," Hamer said.

Then Hamer saw the police take Ponder into custody. "I was holding Miss Ponder's iron," Hamer later told a congressional

THE ROUTE OF THE FREEDOM RIDERS 1961

ATLANTIC OCEAN

GULF OF MEXICO

MAY 4, Departure

Washington, D.C.
Richmond
Petersburg
Lynchburg
Danville
Durham
Rock Hill
Winnsboro
Charlotte
Augusta
Atlanta
Anniston
Montgomery
Birmingham
Meridian
Jackson
New Orleans

MARYLAND
VIRGINIA
WEST VIRGINIA
NORTH CAROLINA
SOUTH CAROLINA
KENTUCKY
TENNESSEE
GEORGIA
ALABAMA
MISSISSIPPI
ARKANSAS
LOUISIANA
FLORIDA

May 7
May 8
May 9
May 10
May 14
May 14
May 20
May 24

N
W   E
S

0   100   200
miles

committee. "I got off to ask her what to do with it. My friends shouted, 'Get back on the bus!'"

But Hamer didn't have time. Another officer arrested her and put her in the car with Ponder. "As I went to get in," Hamer said, "he kicked me. In the car, they would ask me questions. When I started to answer, they would curse and tell me to hush, and call me awful names."

Annelle Ponder and Fannie Lou Hamer were taken to the Montgomery County jail along with five others, including 14-year-old June Johnson and Euvester Simpson. According to Hamer, they were taken to the county jail instead of the city jail so that "we could be far enough out. They didn't care how loud we hollered, wasn't nobody gon' hear us."

Hamer was asked who she was, and where she was from. She told them her name and that she was from Ruleville. "We're going to check that," a state highway patrolman said. Then he went off, and when he came back, he said, "You're damn right. You nigger bitch, we gonna make you wish you was dead."

Later, Hamer concluded that the police had called Ruleville and found out from whites there that she had been organizing blacks to register to vote. "So they was gon' give me as much trouble as possible," she said.

The policemen took June Johnson first and then Annelle Ponder. Hamer later said she could hear the beating and the screams from her cell. When Annelle Ponder was brought back to the cell, Hamer said, "Her eyes looked like blood, and her mouth was swollen. Her clothes were torn. It was horrifying." They took Hamer next.

Hamer remembered:

> One of the men told me, "Get up from there, fatso," and he carried me outa that cell... They had me to lay down on this bunk bed with my face down, and they had two black prisoners. A lot of folks would say, "Well, I woulda died before I'd done that." But nobody know the condition that those prisoners was in before they were s'posed to beat me.

And I heard the highway patrolman tell that black man, said, "If you don't beat her, you know what we'll do to you." And he didn't have no other choice.

While the highway patrolman watched, Hamer recalled, one prisoner beat her with a blackjack (a strip of weighted leather) until he became too tired. Then the other prisoner took over while the first held down Hamer's legs so she couldn't move them.

"I had been beat 'til I was real hard, just hard like a piece of wood or somethin'," Hamer would later say. "A person don't know what can happen to they body if they beat with something like I was beat with."

When word of the arrests reached SNCC, Lawrence Guyot was sent out from Greenwood to see whether he could arrange their release. Instead, he was arrested and beaten, too. The few times that the guards left Hamer's cell door open for some air, she could see Guyot in another cell: "He looked in pretty bad shape. That was the first time I had seen him and not smiling."

Hamer and her group were held in the Winona jail for three days. They didn't hear from anyone and, according to June Johnson, weren't allowed to make any phone calls. "We didn't know what the outcome was going to be," Johnson wrote later.

One time, Hamer overheard a few officers "plotting to kill us, maybe to throw our bodies in the Big Black River, where nobody would ever find us."

Late one night, some policemen offered to let them go, but all seven refused. "I knew it was just so they could kill us and say we was trying to escape. I told 'em they'd have to kill me in my cell," Hamer said.

Finally, James Bevel and Andrew Young of the Southern Christian Leadership Conference (SCLC) were able to arrange for their release with the help of the Justice Department. Young was later to become a U.S. congressman from Georgia, ambassador to the United Nations under President Jimmy Carter, and then mayor of Atlanta.

Hamer had received no medical attention while she was in jail, so Bevel and Young immediately carried her—half conscious and with a Justice Department escort—to a doctor in Greenwood, who stitched her wounds and bandaged her. After that, she was taken to Atlanta for a month to recuperate at the home of some friends of the civil rights movement.

During this month, she refused to let any of her family see her because she had been so badly beaten. In time, the swelling went down, and many of the wounds healed. But Hamer suffered kidney damage that didn't go away, and she developed a blood clot in her left eye that permanently limited her sight.

Hamer also found out when she got out of jail that Medgar Evers had been shot and killed in his own front yard. Evers had been the head of the Mississippi state branch of the NAACP and he had been particularly active in support of James Meredith's case the year before.

In the spring of 1963, Evers had been busy organizing a boycott of segregated stores in the state capital of Jackson, a half-day bus trip south of Ruleville. These were the same stores that were then supporting the White Citizens' Councils. Sit-ins followed, and after the sit-ins, student marchers in early June protested the beating of demonstrators at the sit-ins.

Next came the mass arrests. Jackson's mayor announced that the jails could hold 10,000 demonstrators if necessary. He seemed proud that the city had added more cells since the Freedom Rides.

Jackson's blacks, however, refused to back down, and the situation grew ever more tense as the jails filled and the beatings continued. That summer of 1963, there was a climate of violence in the United States, especially in the South, as though someone's finger were always on a trigger.

June 11 was a particularly fateful day. While Fannie Lou Hamer languished in jail in Mississippi, a lot was happening in Alabama. Governor George Wallace had fulfilled a campaign promise that day to "stand in the schoolhouse door" to prevent integration at the University of Alabama. In response, Presi-

PROTEST DEMONSTRATIONS IN THE SOUTH

Bus Boycott

Demonstrations

Freedom Ride Stop

March

Student Sit-ins

School Integration

★ State Capital

ATLANTIC OCEAN

Washington, D.C.

Richmond ★
VIRGINIA

Raleigh ★
Greensboro
NORTH CAROLINA

Frankfort ★
KENTUCKY

Knoxville
★

Columbia ★
SOUTH
CAROLINA

Nashville
TENNESSEE

St. Augustine
FLORIDA

Memphis

Oxford
MISSISSIPPI

Anniston

Atlanta ★
GEORGIA

Albany

Tallahassee ★

Little Rock ★
ARKANSAS

Meridian

Birmingham

Tuscaloosa
ALABAMA

Selma ★

Montgomery ★

Jackson

Mobile

LOUISIANA

Baton Rouge ★
New Orleans

GULF OF MEXICO

N
W E
S

0   100   200
miles

dent Kennedy had taken over control of the Alabama National Guard and forced Wallace to step aside.

That same night, Kennedy gave a speech to the nation, his strongest yet on the subject of civil rights:

> If an American, because his skin is dark, cannot eat lunch in a restaurant open to the public; if he cannot send his children to the best public school available; if he cannot vote for the public officials who represent him; if, in short, he cannot enjoy the full and free life which all of us want, then who among us would be content to have the color of his skin changed and stand in his place?
>
> Who among us would then be content with the counsels of patience and delay? One hundred years of delay have passed since President Lincoln freed the slaves, yet their heirs, their grandsons, are not fully free. . . .
>
> A great change is at hand, and our task, our obligation, is to make that revolution, that change, peaceful and constructive for all. Those who do nothing are inviting shame as well as violence. Those who act boldly are recognizing right as well as reality.

In Jackson that same night, Medgar Evers was shot in the back as he was returning home. He died one hour later.

Evers was 37 years old at the time. A native Mississippian, he had been born in Decatur, had enlisted in the army in 1943, and then had attended Alcorn Agricultural and Mechanical College after the war. After college, he found work as an insurance salesman before leaving the business world to become a full-time NAACP staffer in 1954.

Evers himself had witnessed terrible racist violence. A close friend of his father's had been lynched when Evers was 14, supposedly for insulting a white woman. "His clothes stayed out in the pasture where they killed him for a long time afterward," Evers later told a reporter from the *New York Times*. "You'd see the blood turning rust color."

On the night of June 11, 1963, Medgar Evers attended a mass

meeting at a local church, then stopped off at the home of a friend. He returned home shortly after midnight. A single round from a high-powered rifle killed Evers on his own front lawn.

The rifle was later recovered, and on it were found the fingerprints of a man named Byron de la Beckwith. Beckwith was a fertilizer salesman from Greenwood and a member of the Greenwood Citizens' Council. He was also as Old South as they came. A hundred years before, his family had been friendly with Confederate President Jefferson Davis.

Beckwith expected a show trial. Instead, he got a surprise: an attempt at justice. The young prosecutor, Bill Waller, had decided to try for a conviction.

Waller's first job was to find jurors who were not prejudiced. He asked one potential juror:

"Do you think it is a crime for a white man to kill a nigger in Mississippi?"

When there was no answer, the judge asked, "What was his answer?"

"He's thinking it over," said Waller. Clearly, just finding people who would be fair jurors was going to be difficult.

The case ended in a mistrial because the all-white jury could not agree on a verdict. Seven jurors voted to free Beckwith. The other five wanted to convict him.

It is a measure of how things were in Mississippi that this split decision was seen as progress. In the Till trial, none of the white jurors had voted to convict.

That same fall of 1963, the Winona policemen who had beaten Hamer and the others were brought to trial in federal district court in Jackson. Students from Ole Miss, still upset over James Meredith's enrollment, filled the courtroom and waved Confederate flags. Finally, the verdict of the all-white jury was read: not guilty. The policemen were acquitted.

"We wondered why we'd come," June Johnson wrote later. "There was no justice."

11 I HAVE A DREAM

66 *I have a dream that one day...even the state of Mississippi, a state sweltering with the heat of injustice, sweltering with the heat of oppression, will be transformed into an oasis of freedom and justice; I have a dream—*

That my four little children will one day live in a nation where they will not be judged by the color of their skin but by the content of their character; I have a dream today. *99*

MARTIN LUTHER KING, JR., at the March on Washington, August 28, 1963

On August 28, 1963, some 200 cars rolled into Washington, D.C., from North Carolina. From New York City, 450 buses came; from Philadelphia, 30,000 people. An 82-year-old man biked to Washington from Ohio. Another man roller-skated from Chicago. Twelve Congress of Racial

Equality (CORE) workers from Brooklyn walked the whole way.

In all, more than 200,000 people came to the nation's capital for the March on Washington that Wednesday. They came to show their support for Martin Luther King, Jr., Fannie Lou Hamer, and the hundreds of other justice seekers in the South. It was the emotional high point of the civil rights movement.

No lunch counters were integrated, and no one was registered to vote, but the joy that people felt that day never left those who were fortunate enough to be there.

That afternoon, Martin Luther King, Jr., gave his famous "I Have a Dream" speech at the Lincoln Memorial and was confirmed as the spiritual leader of the movement. It was the greatest accomplishment of his career, but the road to the Lincoln Memorial had been a difficult one indeed.

Just a few months before, in fact, that road had taken King through Birmingham, Alabama. And in Birmingham, no one was too sure which way the road would turn, toward freedom or toward chaos.

Through the years, Birmingham had become known as one of the country's most racist cities. Not surprisingly, violence was a large part of that reputation. The city was nicknamed "Bombingham" because there had been 50 bombings directed at African Americans since the end of World War II. And Birmingham must have had a very poor police force, because none of these cases was ever solved.

Martin Luther King, Jr., and other representatives of the SCLC came to Birmingham in April 1963 at the request of the Rev. Fred L. Shuttlesworth, of the Sixteenth Street Baptist Church. In 1956, while leading a campaign to desegregate the Birmingham city buses, Shuttlesworth had been awakened one night by a bomb exploding in his house. His church was also bombed, but somehow he survived both incidents. Then in 1957, while attempting to enroll his children in an all-white school, he had been attacked and beaten.

In 1963, things were still very bad in Birmingham, but finally the African-American community had been given a few signs of hope.

The bus terminal attack on the Freedom Riders had deeply embarrassed the city and its business leaders. As a result, Mayor Arthur G. Hanes and his commissioners had been voted out in a special election in November 1962. That election brought in a new mayor and a new system of government. Previously, a board of commissioners had run the city. In April 1963, a new city council would be taking over.

Of the outgoing commissioners, the most notorious was Commissioner of Public Safety T. Eugene "Bull" Connor. In the old system, the police and fire departments were both under Connor's personal control.

Because Connor and Mayor Hanes were both extremists, neither wanted to turn his office over to a racial moderate. So, together, they simply decided not to leave. Shortly after the special election, they declared the results invalid and announced that they would stay on.

This in itself would have been enough to turn city politics upside down. But Birmingham had even more to worry about. Just two weeks before the new city government was to take office, the SCLC began a series of marches and protests against segregation in the downtown stores. The campaign was called Project C. The "C" stood for "confrontation," for coming face-to-face with the people in power.

On April 3, the marches started, as did a boycott of the downtown stores designed to hurt sales during the Easter holiday season. On April 10, a city court issued an order forbidding the marches. King decided to ignore the order and march anyway. That's when the mass arrests started.

On Friday, April 12, Good Friday, King personally led a march, and was arrested by Connor and jailed. On April 15, the new mayor, Albert Boutwell, took over, but the old one, Arthur Hanes, didn't leave. It took one month for a court to rule that Boutwell was the true mayor. In the meantime, Birmingham had two governments, but only one police chief with any power, and that was Connor.

After King was released on bail, he planned the next phase of Project C. The city's police department already had its hands full dealing with the adult marchers. So now King decided to push Birmingham to the breaking point. His scheme was to enlist a new group to join the movement: children.

King realized that schoolchildren could take up just as much space on the streets and in the jails as their parents could. Yet unlike their parents, the children didn't have jobs, so being in jail wouldn't hurt their families economically. Besides, King knew that schoolchildren standing up to policemen would make for powerful pictures on television newscasts.

On Thursday, May 2, 6,000 children entered the struggle. They marched, and 959 were arrested and jailed. The next day, a thousand more showed up at the Sixteenth Street Baptist Church to march.

Angry and frustrated, Bull Connor ordered police dogs and fire hoses to be loosed on the marchers, adults and children alike. It was a big mistake.

Connor's actions made headlines all over the world. Americans saw what he had done on network news programs that night. They saw ferocious police dogs snapping at the heels of young girls, and teenagers being sprayed with jets of water so strong that they knocked the bark off trees.

On Saturday, Connor again used dogs and fire hoses. James Bevel of the SCLC sensed the anger in the marchers. Fearing that a riot might develop, he used a police bullhorn to ask the group to disperse.

Afterward, a brief truce was called. During that truce, Burke Marshall, the assistant attorney general for civil rights, flew in to try to mediate the dispute—that is, to work with both sides to settle the problem. Eleven hundred people had been arrested in the last three days.

On Monday, the marches began again. Everyone was called

out. In one black elementary school, 87 students were present and 1,339 were absent. By Monday night, 2,500 marchers had been arrested, 2,000 of them children. The city and county jails were full.

On May 7, County Sheriff Melvin Bailey met with prominent members of Birmingham's business community. (Because of the confusion in the city government, Birmingham's business leaders were trying to work out their own solution.) Bailey warned them that the local police under Connor were steadily losing control of the situation and that there might be rioting in the streets soon.

Riots, of course, are very bad for business. The businessmen saw that there were only two choices. First, the governor could declare martial law, under which the state police would take over the powers of government. The second choice was to make a deal with King and Shuttlesworth.

Nobody wanted martial law. It would have placed the city under the control of Governor George Wallace, whose segregationist policies were very extreme, even for Birmingham. In the election of 1958, Wallace had lost to John Patterson, a little-known racist, and he had vowed never to forget that loss. "John Patterson out-niggered me," Wallace said after that election. "And boys, I'm not going to be out-niggered again."

Burke Marshall pointed out that dealing with King would be much easier than dealing with rioting black militants. He convinced the business leaders to negotiate. On May 10, a settlement was announced.

The agreement called for lunch-counter and rest-room desegregation within 90 days. Also, the city would begin a policy of nonracial hiring within 60 days, and create fair-employment and biracial committees. Finally, all of the arrested marchers would be released from jail.

With this agreement, both parties hoped the city would calm down. But one day later, the motel where King had been staying and his brother's home were both bombed. Then, when African

Americans took to the streets to protest, they were beaten by Alabama state troopers. In response to these beatings, the riots finally came.

The riots, together with Governor Wallace's performance at the University of Alabama's "schoolhouse door," where he had tried to stop the integration of the university, led to President Kennedy's June 11 speech calling on Congress to enact strong civil rights legislation. One week later he introduced his new civil rights bill to Congress.

King and the other leaders of the movement realized this was a key moment. Something would have to be done to show African-American support for the bill. They decided to stage a massive march on Washington, D.C.

August 28, 1963, was a beautiful day in the District of Columbia, sunny and fresh. The walk from the staging point at the Washington Monument to the Lincoln Memorial, where the program of speeches would be given, was cheerful and calm. The marchers were mostly blacks, but there were also 60,000 whites. There was an atmosphere of unity. Volunteers had even made 80,000 cheese sandwiches in case anyone got hungry.

In the days before the march, the owner of the *Washington Post* had predicted violence and bloodshed. Many government officials were also fearful. They had arranged for 6,000 police to patrol the streets of the capital, with 4,000 troops waiting in reserve.

These fears turned out to be groundless. No police were needed. As *New York Times* reporter Russell Baker commented, "The sweetness and patience of the crowd may have set some sort of national high-water mark in mass decency."

Afterward, in praising the marchers for their "deep fervor" and "quiet dignity," President Kennedy said, "The nation can properly be proud of the demonstration that has occurred here today."

Before the march, Kennedy had been worried about the possibility of violence. But afterward, he turned the event to his own advantage, using the march to urge passage of his civil rights bill.

August 28 was indeed a day of celebration for the civil rights movement. But 18 days later that joy would be turned to sorrow in Birmingham. On Sunday, September 15, 1963, at 10:25 A.M., another bomb ripped through the Sixteenth Street Baptist Church as a children's Bible class was ending.

Gaping holes were blown into the basement wall. Offices in the rear of the church were demolished. Stairways were filled with shattered glass and broken timbers. Four girls from the Bible class were killed by an avalanche of falling bricks and rubble. Fourteen more churchgoers were injured.

The lesson that day had been "The Love That Forgives," but Birmingham's African-American community found it very difficult to forgive this.

Just as they had after the bombing of King's motel the previous May, African Americans took to the streets. Some were so outraged that they even began attacking the police with stones and bricks. The police fought back. The police had guns.

One 16-year-old boy, Johnny Robinson, was shot in the back by a policeman and killed. The officer claimed that Robinson had been throwing rocks at whites who were driving through a black neighborhood waving a Confederate flag.

Another black youth, 13-year-old Virgil Wade, was shot and killed outside Birmingham while riding his bicycle. The police never found the killer. They said "there apparently was no reason at all" for the killing, but suggested that it was related to the riots.

Going from such a high to such a low, all within 18 days, put great pressure on the movement. King and the SCLC continued to preach nonviolence, but more and more African Americans, particularly at SNCC, felt that blacks needed to meet white violence with self-defensive violence of their own.

At the March on Washington, John Lewis of SNCC had originally planned to give a speech criticizing the Kennedy ad-

Martin Luther King, Jr., addresses the March on Washington, August 28, 1963.

ministration for not enforcing the civil rights law. The speech also included a blunt warning to the whites who used hatred and violence: "We shall fragment the South into a thousand pieces, and put them back together again in the image of democracy. We will make the actions of the past few months look pretty."

SNCC workers were being beaten regularly in the South, and Lewis felt that it was important to speak out. But the White House objected to the speech's more threatening passages. The leaders of the march urged Lewis to leave them out, and he finally did.

But keeping those words out of Lewis's speech was not enough to keep those ideas out of the heads of many people in the movement. The idea of "black power" was catching on.

12 MISSISSIPPI SUMMER

> **" Mississippi is unreal when you're not there, and the rest of the country [is] unreal when you are. "**
>
> **ROBERT MOSES**

On January 23, 1964, the civil rights movement won a major victory. The states ratified—that is, agreed to—the 24th Amendment to the Constitution, passed by Congress. This amendment outlawed poll taxes, which had been used to keep poor African Americans from voting. For Fannie Lou Hamer, it was a sign of great hope. The white society in which she lived had always kept her people oppressed. The poll tax was a weapon used against them. Now, at long last, the government seemed to care about justice.

But the leaders of the movement could not afford to rest.

That winter was a time of careful planning, particularly for the leaders of SNCC and CORE.

Earlier that year, SNCC and CORE had formed the Council of Federated Organizations (COFO) to coordinate activities in Mississippi. The SCLC and the NAACP were also part of COFO, but SNCC was in charge. COFO's projects for the summer of 1964 would be the kind of grass-roots work that SNCC favored.

SNCC leaders had two goals. First, they wanted to keep the nation's attention focused on Mississippi. Second, they wanted African Americans in the state to develop their own political groups and leaders.

To achieve these goals, Robert Moses was working closely with Allard Lowenstein, a past leader of the National Student Association. When Moses first asked him to come to Mississippi, Lowenstein was working in New York as a lawyer.

During that trip, Lowenstein told a reporter:

> What we discovered is that the people who run Mississippi today can only do so by force. They cannot allow free elections in Mississippi because if they did, they wouldn't run Mississippi.
>
> And as we go around Mississippi and are arrested and beaten... and threatened and told to leave, we understand why the people asked us to come down here, because inside Mississippi the rule of force is so hard on them that they can't shake the yoke. But when we leave Mississippi we'll tell what we've found, and the people of the United States aren't going to allow this to go on forever.

Many SNCC staffers were becoming increasingly distrustful of whites. Moses, however, still believed firmly in nonviolent integration. He wanted whites and blacks to work together for the cause of justice. Together, he and Lowenstein created what would become the Mississippi Summer Project.

Their plan called for an army of volunteers, mostly from the

North, to descend upon Mississippi the following June. Most of these were to be whites who believed in the movement. There would be teachers, ministers, rabbis, and lawyers. And, of course, there would be students, because they were the ones who always came in large numbers.

If a thousand came, Moses and Lowenstein reasoned, their numbers would be so great that Mississippi could not stop them.

A COFO staff meeting was held on November 14, 1963. Seven white and 35 black field secretaries attended. One of these was Fannie Lou Hamer. She had returned to her duties even before she was properly healed from her beating injuries.

At that meeting, several of the black staffers complained that well-educated whites often took over the programs. Some even said that the role of white volunteers should be restricted so that blacks would not slip into second-class roles. At that point, about 20 percent of the SNCC staff was white.

Moses and Lawrence Guyot, however, defended the white volunteers. Fannie Lou Hamer did, too. She said, "If we're trying to break down this barrier of segregation, we can't segregate ourselves."

Having whites working alongside blacks, Moses said, "changes the whole complexion of what you're doing, so it isn't any longer Negro fighting white. It's rational people fighting against irrational people."

In the end, SNCC and COFO approved the Moses-Lowenstein plan to bring large numbers of whites to Mississippi. Even those who opposed it had to admit that white students would bring national attention. Many of the students would come from prominent families—sons and daughters of congressmen, professors, and so on. Their presence was seen as an opportunity to educate important white northerners about Mississippi.

Also, SNCC depended on northern supporters for money. Its budget was already $750,000, but still funds were so scarce that many staff members had to go without their $10-a-week pay. Having the children of wealth and privilege in Mississippi could only help fundraising efforts. Besides, all the students had agreed to pay their own way. Before the summer began, each committed $150 for traveling expenses and $500 for bail money.

Finally, SNCC felt that white volunteers would be less likely than blacks to encounter violence in Mississippi. This, it turned out, was a terrible mistake.

According to the plan, the white student volunteers would have two tasks. They would help set up Freedom Schools, and they would help with voter-registration drives for the Mississippi Freedom Democratic Party (MFDP).

The Freedom Schools were the idea of Moses himself. Their original purpose was to educate African Americans as voters and train them for leadership roles. But Moses soon realized how poorly the public schools had been educating blacks. Therefore, he expanded the Freedom Schools to include a course in African-American history. There was even a French class, in which Freedom School students learned how to translate "We love freedom."

The main goal of the Mississippi Summer Project, however, was the organization of the MFDP. This new party was supposed to challenge the authority of the white Democratic party in the state.

Even when African Americans were able to register, they were still denied a meaningful vote, because the Mississippi Democrats did not allow African Americans to run for office or vote in the party primaries.

Moses knew that sending student volunteers into rural areas to register blacks would be dangerous. But almost any activity connected with the civil rights movement in Mississippi at that time was dangerous.

Late in the spring of 1964, SNCC and CORE set up a training center in Oxford, Ohio, to introduce volunteers to the ways of Mississippi. The students were warned about the dangers

Robert Moses (left) and James Forman (right) train Summer Project volunteers in Oxford, Ohio.

that might be awaiting them. They were also urged to leave if they had any doubts about their ability to stand the strain.

It was almost like a war, they were told. "Mississippi is unreal when you're not there," Moses said, "and the rest of the country [is] unreal when you are."

Few of the students left, though. For most African Americans in COFO, their training had come during the 1960 sit-ins; for many whites who would later be active in protests against the Vietnam War, that same training came in Mississippi.

After spending the summer of 1964 registering voters in Mississippi, for example, Mario Savio went back to the University of California at Berkeley. There he played a major role in the Berkeley campus revolt known as the Free Speech Movement. The central issue of this protest was the right of students to distribute political pamphlets.

Another student who went to Mississippi that summer was

Andrew Goodman, from Queens College in New York. Goodman left for Mississippi on Saturday, June 20, with the first group of volunteers from Oxford. He was assigned to the CORE office in Meridian, Mississippi. He jumped into the work right away.

That Sunday, June 21, his first full day in Mississippi, Goodman tagged along with two CORE workers who were on their way to Neshoba County, an hour or two away, to investigate a church bombing.

A white New Yorker, Mickey Schwerner had studied at the Columbia University School of Social Work before coming to Mississippi. He was 24 years old, married, and had been with the Meridian CORE office since January. His wife, Rita, was working that summer at the Ohio training center. His close friend, James Chaney, was only 21 years old, but being black and a native Mississippian, he was somewhat more experienced than Schwerner.

Goodman, Schwerner, and Chaney arrived at the site of the bombing without incident. After inspecting what was left of the church, they left at about 3:00 P.M. so that they could get back to Meridian by dinner time. Just outside the town of Philadelphia, though, they were stopped by Deputy Sheriff Cecil Price. He charged them with speeding and took them to the Neshoba County jail in Philadelphia.

At 10:30 that night, without allowing them a phone call, Deputy Price released them. After that, Goodman, Schwerner, and Chaney disappeared.

Because nobody at SNCC had heard from them, and because they had not returned by dinner time, as they had said they would, SNCC headquarters wasted no time in notifying first the Justice Department and then the State Highway Patrol and the FBI.

By six o'clock the next morning, the FBI had entered the case. That same night, the first agents arrived in Philadelphia.

The story was soon on the front page of every newspaper in

the country. As Rita Schwerner pointed out, however, the disappearance would probably have gone unnoticed had only blacks been involved. Five murders of Mississippi blacks that year had already gone unnoticed. Just as Moses and Lowenstein had thought, involving whites in the fight was the key to holding the attention of the press.

The story put immediate pressure on the federal government to find the three missing men. Soon more FBI agents were assigned to the case. Then, four days later, when still no trace had been found, 200 sailors from the Meridian air station were brought in to join the search.

A year earlier in Winona, Fannie Lou Hamer had known better than to leave a Mississippi jail at night. At the training center in Oxford, Ohio, Robert Moses knew, too, that there was very little chance the three civil rights workers were still alive.

Moses had to decide, though, what to tell the volunteers who had not yet left. "We had to tell the students what we thought was going on," he explained later. "Because if, in fact, anyone was arrested and then taken out of jail, then the chances that they were alive were just almost zero. And we had to confront the students with that before they went down, because the ball game was changed."

The disappearance was supposed to scare off the summer volunteers. But it had almost the opposite effect. One white volunteer told a reporter:

> Whenever an incident like this happens, and they happen fairly often, although not usually this serious, everyone reacts the same way. They become more and more determined to stay in the state and fight the evil system that people have to live under here... I'm very much afraid. Everyone here is. But we knew before we came down something about what it's going to be like and I don't know of anybody who's turning back.

All that summer, the volunteers worked under a threat of

violence, and even death. Guns were everywhere. Even movement workers who had once supported the philosophy of non-violence now carried a gun for self-defense.

There seemed to be many good reasons for carrying a gun in Mississippi that summer. There were 35 shooting incidents involving civil rights volunteers. Also, 35 churches and 31 homes belonging to African Americans were either burned or bombed.

For over a month, the search for Goodman, Schwerner, and Chaney continued. But the FBI didn't seem to be getting anywhere. Few in the movement were surprised. FBI chief J. Edgar Hoover had long been deeply suspicious of them. Often when FBI agents had been assigned to investigate racial violence, they investigated the African-American victims instead. Hoover himself claimed that the Communists were behind much of the trouble. Once he called Martin Luther King, Jr., "the most notorious liar in the country."

"Before I became involved in civil rights," Hamer once said, "I would go to the drugstore and I would pick up a detective book or I would pick up a book that said anything about the Justice Department—anything. I thought that was the most fascinating thing I had ever heard about, was the Justice Department and the FBI. Now I wonder who is investigating who, you know?"

Finally, a $25,000 reward offered by the FBI produced some information. On August 4, a tip-off led FBI agents to an earthen dam where the three bodies were found buried in a trench. Goodman and Schwerner, the whites, had been killed with one bullet each. Their black colleague, Chaney, had been beaten and then shot three times. After examining Chaney's body, a coroner from New York said, "In my twenty-five years as a pathologist, I have never witnessed bones so severely shattered."

Still, Mississippi Governor Paul Johnson refused to let the state attorney general bring any charges. It wasn't until December 4 that the Justice Department finally brought charges against 21 men, including Neshoba County Sheriff Lawrence Rainey and Deputy Sheriff Cecil Price. Because the federal government cannot bring criminal murder counts, the men were charged instead with violations of the civil rights code, specifically the violation of every American's right to live.

At the trial of the 18 who were eventually indicted—that is, officially accused of a crime—the full story finally came out. Before Price had released Goodman, Schwerner, and Chaney, he had arranged for some local Ku Klux Klan members to intercept the three civil rights workers as they left Philadelphia. After a wild car chase, the three men were caught and then killed.

When the verdict came down, Rainey and ten others were freed, but Price and six others were found guilty and received sentences ranging from 3 to 10 years. It was the first time in Mississippi history that an all-white jury had convicted white defendants in a civil rights case.

The parents of Mickey Schwerner and James Chaney decided to have their sons' bodies buried side by side. But the state of Mississippi refused to allow it. Like its bus stations and its restaurants, its libraries and its movie theaters, Mississippi's cemeteries were also segregated.

13 IS THIS AMERICA?

66 *We didn't come all this way for no two seats when all of us is tired.* 99

FANNIE LOU HAMER, at the 1964 Democratic National Convention

Organizing and registering African Americans in Mississippi was a dangerous job. The experiences of the Mississippi Summer Project volunteers had shown that. They had also shown how brave Fannie Lou Hamer had been to continue her tireless work in the churches and in the fields of rural Mississippi organizing the Mississippi Freedom Democratic Party (MFDP).

To the white Mississippians who ran the state, lunch counters were one thing, and voting rights were another. Allard Lowenstein knew this. If the whites who ran Mississippi ever allowed free elections, he once said, they wouldn't be running Mississippi anymore.

Many whites in the state feared the power of black voters. To be seen even talking to a Council of Federated Organizations (COFO) worker could lead to being fired, beaten, or maybe even killed.

In spite of this danger, the MFDP, founded on April 26, in Jackson, was organized during the summer of 1964. By the time its state convention was held in Jackson in August, 60,000 members had already been signed up.

In many ways, the MFDP was a last resort. Hamer and other African Americans had tried to work within the state Democratic party, but had been turned away. Often the state party kept African Americans out by holding party meetings in private homes and keeping the time and place secret.

Because the regular Democratic party wouldn't let them in, Mississippi's blacks formed their own, integrated party. Their plan was to challenge the regular party's right to represent Mississippi at the Democratic National Convention in Atlantic City that August.

At the MFDP's own state convention in August, 64 blacks and 4 whites were chosen to represent the party in Atlantic City. A white minister, Edwin King, was elected chairman of the delegation. Fannie Lou Hamer was elected vice-chairman. For Hamer, this was a great honor. It showed how important she had become to the civil rights movement in Mississippi.

When President Lyndon B. Johnson heard that the MFDP would be coming to Atlantic City, he was furious. His greatest concern was to beat the Republican candidate, Senator Barry Goldwater, in the fall election. President Johnson worried that the MFDP would disrupt party unity at the convention.

Johnson had expected to be the choice of supporters of the civil rights movement. In the last year, he had fought a difficult battle to win support for the Civil Rights Act of 1964. The people who had fought hardest against the bill were the same ones now supporting Goldwater.

The Civil Rights Act of 1964 was an even stronger version of the bill that President Kennedy had proposed the year before.

Johnson's new bill was a great victory for the civil rights movement. It clearly outlawed all racial discrimination in public places such as restaurants, bus stations, and motels, ending Jim Crow forever.

However, many African Americans, including those in the MFDP, weren't satisfied. The new law did little to help promote black voting rights. After all, to obtain voting rights was the reason that the MFDP had been created in the first place.

As the summer went on, a few SNCC leaders worked behind the scenes to convince other state delegations to support the MFDP at the convention. Many other SNCC workers, though, had lost faith in the national political system. They didn't believe that the MFDP could succeed. But when the large and influential New York delegation announced its support of the MFDP, even the most gloomy SNCC staffers were encouraged.

In the White House, President Johnson was getting nervous. He believed that a fight on the convention floor over the MFDP could cost him southern support. To stop that, he took several steps to control the MFDP.

One of these steps was to have J. Edgar Hoover's FBI keep a watch on SNCC and the MFDP. The FBI bugged the telephones in SNCC's Atlantic City offices. Johnson also began putting pressure on white supporters of the MFDP.

The strange thing about Johnson's action was that the MFDP was just about his only political support in the Deep South. In supporting the regular party, he was turning against the one group of Mississippians who had remained loyal to him and to the Democratic party.

The president seemed to be acting foolishly, but this was not surprising from the viewpoint of the civil rights movement. Like Eisenhower and Kennedy before him, Johnson was afraid of acting in support of African Americans because he feared the loss of political support. It was a lesson the movement had finally learned: National political leaders often could not be trusted to help African Americans win their rights. In the end, blacks would have to win that fight themselves.

The MFDP delegation left for Atlantic City during the second week of August. For many in the delegation, it was their first trip outside Mississippi. For all of them, it was the moment toward which they had been working all summer.

By the time the delegation arrived in Atlantic City, the MFDP had won the support of 9 state delegations, 25 congressmen, and the powerful United Auto Workers union.

The MFDP's goal was to be seated as Mississippi's legal delegation. This meant that the Democratic Party's Credentials Committee would have to recognize them. The MFDP didn't have enough support to win the vote in the Credentials Committee itself, because most of the votes there were controlled by President Johnson. But if the MFDP could get just 11 votes on the 108-member committee, then the fight would go to the convention floor. And there the MFDP felt it could win.

Before the convention, the MFDP thought it had more than the 11 votes it needed. But then President Johnson went to work. His expected running mate, Hubert Humphrey, had been a longtime supporter of the civil rights cause. Humphrey had many friends among the moderates in the movement. As the convention was about to begin, Johnson told Humphrey that if he wanted to be vice president he would have to stop the MFDP.

Johnson's people also began threatening Credentials Committee members who supported the MFDP. According to MFDP lawyer Joseph Rauh, one black California supporter was told "that her husband wouldn't get a judgeship if she didn't leave us, and the Secretary of the Army told the guy from the Canal Zone that he would lose his job if he didn't leave us."

On Saturday, August 22, the Credentials Committee met before a national television audience to hear the MFDP's case. Hamer gave her famous testimony. She described the hard life of African Americans in Mississippi. She told how they were kept out of the political process. Then she told the story of her beating in the Winona jail. When she was finished, she chal-

Two Seats:
The Atlantic City Convention

The Atlantic City convention was supposed to be a smooth and happy one for the Democratic Party. Lyndon Johnson would be nominated to run for another four years as president. Hubert Humphrey would be his running mate. But neither Johnson nor Humphrey had counted on the Mississippi Freedom Democratic party (MFDP).

Johnson had thought that signing the Civil Rights Act of 1964, which outlawed Jim Crow segregation in the South, would be enough to satisfy southern blacks. It wasn't. Johnson then decided the the MFDP could not be allowed to disrupt party unity at the convention. He would try to make a deal. The deal Johnson wanted to make gave the 68 MFDP delegates only two at-large seats. After an emotional speech by Fannie Lou Hamer, however, the MFDP rejected the compromise. "We didn't come all this way for no two seats when all of us is tired," Hamer said.

Lyndon Johnson went to Atlantic City knowing that he would win the presidential nomination.

Police prevent MFDP delegates from entering the convention hall in Atlantic City.

MFDP delegates take their seats on the convention floor: Annie Devine, Fannie Lou Hamer, and Edwin King.

lenged the committee to do the right thing.

"If the Freedom Democratic Party is not seated now," Hamer declared in a voice filled with conviction, "I question America. Is this America, the land of the free and the home of the brave, where we have to sleep with our telephones off of the hook because our lives be threatened daily, because we want to live as decent human beings in America?"

President Johnson was afraid that MFDP testimony such as Hamer's would capture the public's heart. He made a last-minute request for television air time. In the middle of the hearing, the networks all switched over to the president's news conference.

This trick cut off coverage of MFDP testimony, but not before Hamer had said what she had come to say. Enough got through to move the nation. The next day viewers from all over the country sent telegrams to their delegates urging support of the MFDP.

Johnson now had to deal even more forcefully with the situation. He had Humphrey name Walter Mondale, a follower of Humphrey and later a vice president himself, to negotiate a settlement.

Mondale worked out a deal that called for the seating of every Mississippi regular who would sign a party loyalty oath. Also, there would be two at-large seats for the MFDP. Finally, the national party would pledge that no segregated delegations would be seated at the 1968 convention.

Mondale found the problem so difficult to solve because there was no middle ground. He couldn't give a little here and take a little there, as was usually the case with political solutions, because the issue was black and white, morality versus politics. Either the MFDP deserved to represent Mississippi and its 850,000 blacks, or it didn't. The convention had to either accept that claim or reject it. If the MFDP claim was just, how could the white regulars be seated at all?

The civil rights movement had found itself in this situation many times before. Many times since the 1955 Montgomery bus boycott, the Rev. Dr. Martin Luther King, Jr., had run into the same problem. Sometimes he had been able to shame whites into change; other times, he had not.

Meanwhile, though, Johnson kept up his pressure on the MFDP. He had reduced its support on the Credentials Committee to just four votes, which was not enough to bring the issue to the floor. Now he called on Humphrey and other leaders to convince the MFDP to accept Mondale's plan.

On August 25, King and Bayard Rustin, the master organizer of the March on Washington, arranged for Humphrey to meet with Robert Moses, who was heading the COFO staff at the convention. Moses, of course, had great influence with the MFDP delegation. He listened politely to what Humphrey had to say. But the senator from Minnesota was unable to persuade Moses to change his mind and support the Mondale plan.

President Johnson then called on Walter Reuther, leader of the United Auto Workers union, to use his influence with Rauh. At the time, Rauh was on the UAW payroll, so he listened very carefully to what Reuther had to say. Like many white liberal supporters of the civil rights movement, Rauh had other concerns as well.

On August 26, the night before the convention officially opened, the MFDP held a final meeting to decide whether or not to accept the two-seat offer. King, Rustin, and Rauh all spoke in favor of accepting the compromise. Moses told the delegation that the COFO staff was against it, but that they should make up their own minds because that's what voting was all about.

Finally, Fannie Lou Hamer spoke.

Earlier that evening, Hamer had gone to Moses to ask his advice. "I went to Bob," she would say later.

> I was desperate. I asked him, "What in the world should we do?" I said, "I believe it's wrong for us to accept a compromise...But do you think we ought to accept it?"
>
> He said, "You grown. You make your own decision."
>
> Then I said, "I'm going to make it even if it is wrong."

Hamer spoke against the compromise so strongly that the rest of the delegation voted to reject it. As she said, "We didn't come all this way for no two seats when all of us is tired."

The next day, in 30 seconds, the Democratic delegates approved of the deal. The business of the convention went on. Johnson received the presidential nomination, and Humphrey was nominated for vice president. But in the MFDP delegation, and in the civil rights movement at large, there was great bitterness.

The MFDP delegates and other civil rights leaders believed that the white liberals had sold them out. Even though all but three of the white regulars had walked out, the two at-large seats were not enough for the MFDP. The at-large label meant that the convention had not recognized the MFDP's right to represent Mississippians.

"We followed all the laws that the white people themselves made," Hamer said.

> We tried to attend the precinct meetings and they locked the doors on us or moved the meetings—and that's against the laws they made for their own selves.
>
> So we were the ones that held the real precinct meetings. At all these meetings across the state we elected our representatives to go to the National Convention in Atlantic City. But we learned the hard way that even though we had all the law and all the righteousness on our side, that the white man is not going to give up his power to us.

The defeat was especially hard on Robert Moses, who had worked so hard to bring blacks and whites together that summer. After the convention, Moses left the MFDP. He no longer believed that there was any point to working within the Democratic party. What good was the right to vote in Democratic primaries if the party did nothing to guarantee African Americans the right to register to vote.

To the radicals in SNCC, the convention was just more proof that the power to vote meant nothing. To them, the whole system was corrupt. True, the MFDP experiment proved that blacks could organize and work within the political system. But it also proved to many that, as Fannie Lou Hamer said, "the white man is not going to give up his power to us."

Nineteen sixty-four was a time of increasing black-white tension in the country and in the movement. It was also the last summer that blacks and whites would work together on such a massive scale.

In the November 1964 election, Johnson won by a landslide, as had been expected. Also as had been expected, Goldwater carried the Deep South easily. Despite its treatment at the convention, the MFDP was just about the only political group in Mississippi to remain loyal to the Democratic party.

SNCC field-worker and MFDP delegate Unita Blackwell remembered:

> The whole issue around the compromise for us, and for me, was that it was some kind of political ploy that [the northern politicians] understood. But for us, for Mississippi, it was what was right and what was wrong.
>
> We had been done wrong. Our rights had been taken away. And you just couldn't issue some two seats at large to correct that.

The experience of the MFDP at the Atlantic City convention frustrated many people who had sacrificed so much for so long. But the failure of the MFDP delegation to be seated did not mean that the challenge was itself a failure.

Though it was not apparent at the time, the MFDP's heroic effort ensured that the Democratic party would in the future open itself up to African Americans. It also showed the nation that southern blacks were being denied the voting rights they so clearly deserved.

14 THE LAST MARCH

> ❝ *Stronger than all the armies is an idea whose time has come.* ❞
>
> **SENATOR EVERETT DIRKSEN, on the passage of the Civil Rights Act of 1964**

In the 10 years after the *Brown* decision was handed down in 1954, the civil rights movement had committed itself to Martin Luther King, Jr.'s philosophy of nonviolence. That philosophy had successfully brought southern blacks out of a Jim Crow world. It had led them into a world of integrated lunch counters and open schoolhouse doors. Many other doors, however, remained locked and barred.

To some young African Americans within the movement, the time for nonviolence had passed. They were living each day under the threat of violence and death. The gentle nature of nonviolent civil disobedience seemed almost silly to them. Some began carrying guns. Others argued for violent clashes with the whites who were keeping blacks down.

During the summer of 1964, there were race riots in Harlem, Chicago, and Philadelphia. The Harlem riot was sparked when an off-duty white policeman shot and killed a 15-year-old black. The policeman claimed the boy had threatened him with a knife. But it wasn't the boy's death alone that caused the riot. These riots were already waiting to happen. A year later, for instance, the Watts riot in Los Angeles, the biggest riot by far, was started by a minor traffic arrest for drunk driving.

The same sort of frustrations could also be found in the South. As 1965 began, radicals in SNCC began to challenge Martin Luther King, Jr., for leadership of the movement.

The radicals had experience organizing door-to-door in the Deep South. This had brought them face-to-face with the brutality of the whites resisting change. As a result, SNCC radicals wanted their freedom, and they wanted it now, at any cost, even at the cost of their own lives. If they had to die, they wanted to die fighting.

Some SNCC leaders went so far as to form an alliance with Malcolm X, the northern black activist who had become famous for preaching violence as a means of self-defense. Later, when these same SNCC leaders began urging the African-American community to rise up, it was clear what they had in mind.

At that point, no one either within the movement or without knew which philosophy would prevail: violence or nonviolence.

In Selma, Alabama, SNCC workers had been helping the local residents organize and register voters for more than three years. Lately, though, SNCC efforts had begun to weaken. There had been the usual resistance and arrests, of course. But what had really hurt SNCC were its money problems. Also the SNCC staffers were tired and worn down.

Grass-roots organizing was SNCC's specialty, and its great contribution to the movement. But Selma's African-American leaders grew worried that all the work of the past years would be lost. So in January 1965, they called on Martin Luther King, Jr., and the SCLC for help.

By that time, SNCC and SCLC had developed a strong rivalry. King gave a speech in Selma announcing "the beginning of a determined, organized, mobilized campaign." But instead of being pleased, SNCC workers were furious because King seemed to be saying that their efforts had been shallow and disorganized.

SNCC believed firmly in simple local organizing. To most of its staff, King was too flashy, always jetting from one trouble spot to another, always bringing the press along with him. Just one month earlier, King had been in Oslo, Norway, to accept the Nobel Peace Prize; next month, who could say where he would be? SNCC, however, was in Selma to stay.

SNCC knew that King could bring money and attention to a community. But SNCC's leaders had long been concerned with what happened to organizing efforts after the great leader left. Too many times before, they had seen that the letdown was often crushing.

Also, SNCC was made up mostly of eager young men who lived in the local communities where they worked. They believed strongly in working from the bottom up. The SCLC, however, was a smaller band of experienced professionals who traveled around to those places where they believed they were needed most.

It was natural that the two groups would disagree. In Selma, however, for the sake of the community, they tried at first to put aside their differences and work together. That campaign began on January 18, 1965, with a series of marches to the courthouse.

Selma's mayor, Joseph Smitherman, was young and inexperienced. Its county sheriff, Jim Clark, was widely known to have a bad temper. In fact, movement leaders were counting on Sheriff Clark's temper to start enough trouble so that the federal government in Washington would be forced to get involved.

As he often did, King looked at things from a national perspective. He hoped that a success in Selma would speed passage of the new voting rights legislation that had recently been proposed by President Johnson.

But Mayor Smitherman, though inexperienced, was also smart. He understood what the movement was trying to do, and he did his best to avoid trouble. He had learned the lessons of Jackson and of Birmingham, that giving in to frustration always costs in the end.

For all his shrewdness, however, Smitherman could not control Sheriff Clark. And Clark could not control his own temper.

During one of the first protests, Clark arrested Amelia Boynton, a respected community leader. Some 105 teachers marched to the courthouse in response, even though they knew the white school board might use the march as cause to dismiss them.

Teachers in the South held a respected place in the community. Once they marched, other groups did, too. The morticians organized a march, and so did the beauticians. Middle-class Selma was on the move.

It was clear that some momentum for change was growing in Selma, but Clark stood firm. It was yet another case of an irresistible force meeting an immovable object.

SNCC and the SCLC both believed in engagement, and engage Jim Clark they did. In early 1965, there were 3,300 arrests.

Meanwhile, there was trouble in nearby Marion, Alabama. A nighttime march on February 18 ended in beatings and death when a white mob, including some police, attacked the crowd.

While protecting his mother from assault, Jimmy Lee Jackson, a veteran registration worker, was shot at point-blank range by an Alabama state trooper. He died seven days later.

Jackson's SNCC colleagues were both upset and angry. Some talked of taking his body to Governor George Wallace in Montgomery and leaving it on the steps of the state capitol. Others spoke of getting their guns. The death of Jimmy Lee Jackson was such an outrage that something had to be done.

"When you have a great violation of the people," the Rev. James Bevel of the SCLC explained, "when there's a great sense of injury, you have to give people an honorable means and context in which to express and eliminate that grief, and speak decisively and succinctly back to the issue. Otherwise, your movement will break down into violence and chaos."

King and the SCLC decided to stage a symbolic 54-mile march from Selma to the state capitol in Montgomery. This march would use up the energy and emotion created by Jackson's murder. It would also focus national attention on the issue during the five days the march would take.

SNCC objected to the plan. The march would be dangerous, and SNCC always favored careful organization over SCLC-style showmanship. Governor Wallace also objected, announcing that he would prevent the march.

Despite SNCC's objections and Wallace's ban, however, 600 marchers headed out of Selma on Sunday, March 7. King was off preaching in Atlanta, so the group was led by Hosea Williams of the SCLC and SNCC chairman John Lewis. Lewis was marching even though his organization officially refused to participate.

No police stopped the group as it moved through the center of town. But at the Edmund Pettus Bridge, which led out of Selma, state troopers were waiting.

As the marchers began to cross the bridge, the state police, under orders from Wallace, directed the crowd to break up. When the marchers held their ground, the state police, in full riot gear, began to advance, at first slowly but then at a run. Tear-gas grenades exploded, clouding the scene. Then the beatings began. State policemen on horseback galloped through the streets, swinging at anything that moved.

That night, all three networks interrupted their prime-time programming to show footage from the Edmund Pettus Bridge. The film clips they showed looked like war on the streets of Selma. The police wore strange, bug-eyed gas masks. A fog of tear gas hid the marchers. The scene looked like a bad science-fiction movie. Once again, the nation was outraged by white brutality in the South.

In the African-American community, shock quickly gave way to anger and talk of getting even. SNCC now insisted on a march to show that the African Americans of Selma would not back down.

A call went out to friends of the movement for help. Hundreds, both black and white, poured into Selma in response. Over 450 members of the clergy came. So did Fannie Lou Hamer.

Black leaders were especially concerned that whites be included in the marches. They feared that the National Guard would not be called out to protect only blacks.

In the meantime, a federal judge in Montgomery issued an order forbidding the march until a hearing could be held. King had never before violated a federal court order, and he didn't want to take that step now. But the momentum was growing, and pressure from SNCC was great. On Tuesday, March 9, two days after Bloody Sunday, King personally led a crowd of 2,000 marchers across the Edmund Pettus Bridge.

Once again, Alabama state troopers were there to block the way. Having been reprimanded by Governor Wallace for their violence two days before, the troopers did not attack right away. But King did not want to test them. Nor did he want to test the federal court order. Instead, he knelt, led the marchers in a prayer, and then turned the column of people around.

SNCC leaders couldn't believe it. They called King's actions a "sellout." But the SCLC defended King. It pointed out that to have continued the march would have given the police an excuse to beat the marchers "with court approval."

King asked the out-of-town marchers to stay on in Selma while he attempted to have the court order lifted. Many had come without even a toothbrush, assuming that they would be needed only for the day. But many stayed on anyway. One of those who stayed was James Reeb, a white Unitarian minister from Boston.

That night, Reeb and two other white ministers accidentally wandered into a white segregationist neighborhood. All three men were attacked, and Reeb had his head beaten in with a club. He died two days later. The nation mourned his death, but African Americans in SNCC were disturbed that Reeb's death had shaken the country whereas Jimmy Lee Jackson's had not.

Finally, a week later, the court order was lifted. On Sunday, March 21, two weeks after Bloody Sunday, King led 3,200 marchers across the Edmund Pettus Bridge and out of Selma. When asked how he felt about the marchers, Sheriff Clark said he was glad to see them go.

Martin Luther King, Jr., (left) and Ralph Abernathy (right) on the second day of the Selma march.

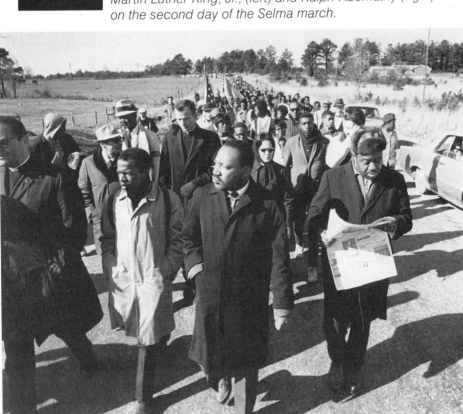

By the time King arrived in Montgomery five days later, he was leading a column of people 25,000 strong. It was a triumphant return to the city in which he had begun his work nearly 10 years before. So much had changed, so much was different. In the joy of the moment, who would have thought that this would be the last dramatic act of the traditional civil rights movement?

The march from Selma was the last act of the unified group of blacks and whites, radicals and moderates, who together formed the civil rights movement. After Selma, it was pulled apart. Or rather, it pulled itself apart.

Yet Selma was still a great victory. It helped bring speedy passage of the Voting Rights Act of 1965, which President Johnson signed into law on August 6. That act set up a system of federal examiners to make sure that no eligible citizen was denied the right to vote. The 24th Amendment had already outlawed the poll tax; now the Voting Rights Act outlawed the literacy test and other unfair barriers to the registration of African Americans. Specifically, the act banned discrimination in federally aided programs. It also ordered the U.S. attorney general to bring lawsuits against local poll taxes.

In Selma in January 1965, over 50 percent of the population was black, but less than one percent of them were registered to vote. With the help of the Voting Rights Act of 1965, SNCC was able to register 9,000 of Selma's black citizens in less than a year.

For Fannie Lou Hamer, the Voting Rights Act was particularly meaningful. She herself had struggled to beat the racist literacy test. Now, at long last, her efforts had paid off. The law of the land had been changed.

15 RULEVILLE IS MY HOME

> **❝** *I have a right to stay here. With all that my parents and grandparents gave to Mississippi, I have a right to stay here and fight for what they didn't get.* **❞**

FANNIE LOU HAMER

After the Democratic National Convention in Atlantic City, Fannie Lou Hamer joined a SNCC delegation that made a tour of black-governed African countries in the fall of 1964. In Africa, for the first time in her life, she saw blacks doing things that in the United States she had only seen whites do.

Hamer said later:

> Being from the South, we never was taught much about our African heritage. The way everybody talked to us, everybody in Africa was savages and real stupid people.

But I've seen more savage white folks here in America than I seen in Africa.

I saw black men flying the airplanes, driving the buses, sitting behind the big desks in the bank, and just doing everything that I was used to seeing white people do.

Hamer was particularly impressed by the president of Guinea, Sekou Touré. Rather than wait for the SNCC delegates to come to the presidential palace, Touré himself came to visit them at their hotel.

After the trip to Africa, Hamer returned to Ruleville, to her own people, to organize. Many of her friends in SNCC were moving away from Democratic party politics in favor of something more radical. But Hamer stayed committed to the political process.

As part of the Mississippi Summer Project, she ran for Congress against a white congressman, James Whitten. She ran in a special counter-election held by SNCC. In the all-white regular Democratic party primary, only Whitten's name had been listed on the ballot; in the SNCC election, however, both names were listed.

Whitten won one election, and Hamer won the other. In January 1965, she and two other MFDP congressional candidates, Victoria Gray and Annie Devine, traveled to Washington to press their claims. They were not seated, however. As a delaying tactic, the case was sent to the House Subcommittee on Elections where it was to be investigated.

On September 17, after nine months of investigation, the full House voted on the matter. The MFDP claim was defeated by 85 votes. But some progress was made. Over 15,000 pages of evidence were produced for the subcommittee hearings. Thanks to that work, the elections in Mississippi were eventually ruled illegal by the federal courts.

The mid-1960s were a time of great change in the civil rights movement. Radical blacks in SNCC rejected white volunteers and staff members. They then turned further toward violence, feeling the same sort of anger that later led to the formation of the Black Panther party.

These African Americans believed that the federal government and northern whites would act only against extreme prejudice in the South. They felt that less obvious, but still damaging aspects of racism in the North were overlooked. It made them angry.

Even Martin Luther King, Jr., couldn't escape the violence that was shaking the United States. On April 3, 1968, King traveled to Memphis, Tennessee, to lead a peaceful march of striking sanitation workers. On April 4, while standing on the balcony of the Lorraine Motel, he was shot and killed by a white man named James Earl Ray. Ray was later caught and sentenced to 99 years in prison.

King's death was a great loss to the movement. But great losses often give way to great gains. Three days after King's death, Congress passed the Civil Rights Act of 1968, which outlawed discrimination in the sale and rental of housing. The act was a tribute to King.

Later that same year, in August 1968, Hamer again traveled to the Democratic National Convention. This time the convention was held in Chicago. This time Hamer came as a member of the Mississippi Loyalist Democratic party (MLDP). And this time she won.

In between the two conventions, and thanks in part to Hamer's exhaustive work, the MFDP had become strong. It was now established enough to attract sympathetic white members of the regular party. Eventually, the MFDP took a new name to reflect this expanded membership. It was now called the Mississippi Loyalist Democratic party.

The regulars were the same old segregationists, though, and at Chicago there was another battle before the Credentials Committee. The committee wanted to compromise again by seating 21 members of each delegation. But just as the MFDP had remained firm four years before, the MLDP stood its ground, too, and refused to compromise.

This time, the strategy worked. The regulars were unseated altogether. But the regulars refused to leave. There were shouts of "Unconstitutional!" and "Illegal!" Tempers rose again.

On the stage, however, the chairman of the Credentials Committee calmly pointed to a piece of paper. On it was the 1964 order to integrate. Immediately the shouts of the segregationists were drowned out by cries of "Free at last!" and "We shall overcome!"

Fannie Lou Hamer gestures in her speech to the 1968 Democratic National Convention.

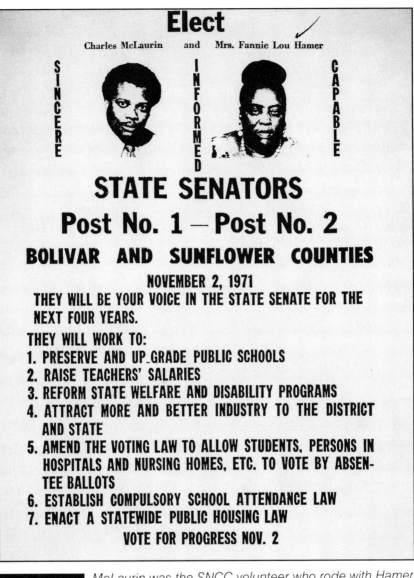

Elect

Charles McLaurin and Mrs. Fannie Lou Hamer

S I N C E R E

I N F O R M E D

C A P A B L E

STATE SENATORS
Post No. 1 — Post No. 2

BOLIVAR AND SUNFLOWER COUNTIES

NOVEMBER 2, 1971

THEY WILL BE YOUR VOICE IN THE STATE SENATE FOR THE NEXT FOUR YEARS.

THEY WILL WORK TO:
1. PRESERVE AND UP-GRADE PUBLIC SCHOOLS
2. RAISE TEACHERS' SALARIES
3. REFORM STATE WELFARE AND DISABILITY PROGRAMS
4. ATTRACT MORE AND BETTER INDUSTRY TO THE DISTRICT AND STATE
5. AMEND THE VOTING LAW TO ALLOW STUDENTS, PERSONS IN HOSPITALS AND NURSING HOMES, ETC. TO VOTE BY ABSENTEE BALLOTS
6. ESTABLISH COMPULSORY SCHOOL ATTENDANCE LAW
7. ENACT A STATEWIDE PUBLIC HOUSING LAW

VOTE FOR PROGRESS NOV. 2

McLaurin was the SNCC volunteer who rode with Hamer to Indianola on her first trip to register.

When Fannie Lou Hamer finally took her seat at the convention she received a standing ovation.

Hamer would remain active in Democratic party politics for the rest of her life. She served on the party's ruling body, the Democratic National Committee, from 1968 until 1971. As late as 1976, when her health began failing, she was still working tirelessly to unite the blacks and whites of Mississippi into one integrated party.

In the years after the 1968 Chicago convention, Hamer also worked to solve the problems of Ruleville's poor. In fact, she, who had always devoted her time and energy to the community, was still poor herself.

Over the next 10 years, Hamer organized more poverty programs, raised money for low-income housing, started a day-care center that still bears her name, and made plans for a garment factory to provide jobs for Ruleville residents. She also ran (unsuccessfully) for the Mississippi state senate in 1971, along with Charles McLaurin, one of the SNCC workers who had traveled with her to Indianola on that first registration bus trip some nine years before.

Hamer's most cherished project, though, was the Freedom Farm Cooperative.

Fannie Lou Hamer liked to say that "if you give a hungry man food, he will eat it. [But] if you give him land, he will grow his own food." And that's exactly what over 5,000 people did on the 680 acres of Freedom Farm: they grew their own food.

When Hamer started the Freedom Farm Cooperative, she had just 40 acres. But on her speaking trips around the country, she would talk up the project and ask for donations. Soon offers of help were coming from all over. In Chicago, 176,000 white high school students walked on a March Against Hunger to raise funds for the Freedom Farm.

Then on March 14, 1977, Fannie Lou Hamer died of cancer. She was not yet 60 years old. And sadly, the Freedom Farm died along with her, unable to support itself without Hamer's vigor and vigilance to give it strength.

Like the civil rights movement itself, Fannie Lou Hamer's life was filled with both victories and defeats. Also like the movement itself, she kept on fighting regardless of the difficulties.

Her strength and her conviction had carried her all the way from the cotton fields of the Mississippi Delta to the halls of power in Atlantic City. Sometimes along the way she had been afraid, but never had she given in to her fear.

Hamer (left) and two other MFDP congressional candidates before losing their bid to be seated.

Like James Meredith, Medgar Evers, and Robert Moses, Fannie Lou Hamer was a hero to everyone in the nation who sympathized with the struggle of African Americans for their basic civil rights. Her work showed what just one courageous person could achieve. Like so many others whose stories were never told, Hamer was willing to sacrifice, and even die, for the movement if, in the end, the world would be a better place for what she had done. She simply did what she thought was right.

For all her triumphs and defeats, it is perhaps best to remember Fannie Lou Hamer as she was in June 1964, at the brink of the Mississippi Freedom Summer. That was a time when the only people who had ever heard of Andrew Goodman, Mickey Schwerner, and James Chaney were their friends and families.

Sally Belfrage was a student volunteer that summer, and in her book, *Freedom Summer*, she wrote of seeing Fannie Lou Hamer for the first time:

> Then there was a change: a woman whose badge read "Mrs. Fannie Lou Hamer" was suddenly leading [the students], molding their noise into music.
>
> Her voice gave everything she had, and her circle soon incorporated the others, expanding first in size and in volume and then something else—it gained passion. Few of them knew who she was, and in her plump, perspiring face many could probably see something of the woman who cleaned their mothers' floors at home.
>
> But here was clearly someone with force enough for all of them, who knew the meaning of "Oh Freedom" and "We Shall Not Be Moved" in her flesh and spirit as they never would. They lost their shyness and began to sing the chorus with abandon, though their voices all together dimmed beside hers.

Timetable of Events in the Life of
Fannie Lou Hamer

October 6, 1917	Born in Montgomery County, Mississippi
1923	Starts working in the fields
1929	Leaves school to work full-time Joins Stranger's Home Baptist Church
1944	Marries Perry "Pap" Hamer Attends mass meeting organized by SCIC and SNCC Fails voter registration literacy test Shot at for trying to register to vote
1963	Successfully registers to vote on third attempt Arrested and severely beaten in Winona, Mississippi
1964	Elelcted vice-chairman, MFDP Testifies before Democratic National Convention in Atlantic City
1968	Receives standing ovation as she takes her seat at Democratic National Convention in Chicago Elected Democratic national committeewoman
1969	Founds Freedom Farm Cooperative
1971	Runs unsuccessfully for Mississippi State Senate
March 15, 1977	Dies of cancer in Mound Bayou, Mississippi

SUGGESTED READING

Belfrage, Sally. *Freedom Summer.* New York: Viking, 1968.

Branch, Taylor. *Parting the Waters: America in the King Years, 1954–63.* New York: Simon and Schuster, 1988.

Freedman, Florence. *Two Tickets to Freedom.* New York: Bedrick Books, 1989.

*Kling, Susan. *Fannie Lou Hamer.* Chicago: Salsedo Press, 1979.

Leuchtenburg, William E. *A Troubled Feast: American Society Since 1945.* Boston: Little, Brown and Company, 1979.

Lewis, Anthony, and *The New York Times. Portrait of a Decade: The Second American Revolution.* New York: Random House, 1964.

*Raines, Howell. *My Soul Is Rested: Movement Days in the Deep South.* New York: Putnam's, 1977.

Von Hoffman, Nicholas. *Mississippi Notebook.* New York: David White, 1964.

Williams, Juan. *Eyes on the Prize.* New York: Viking, 1987.

*Readers of *Fannie Lou Hamer: From Sharecropping to Politics* will find these books particularly readable.

SOURCES

Belfrage, Sally. *Freedom Summer.* New York: Viking, 1968.

Carson, Clayborne. *In Struggle: SNCC and the Black Awakening of the 1960s.* Cambridge, Mass.: Harvard University Press, 1981.

Eyes on the Prize. Boston: Blackside, Inc., 1987. Video.

Hofstadter, Richard et al. *The United States.* Englewood Cliffs, N.J.: Prentice-Hall, 1976.

Jones, Jacqueline. *Labor of Love, Labor of Sorrow.* New York: Basic Books, 1985.

Kling, Susan. *Fannie Lou Hamer.* Chicago: Salsedo Press, 1979.

Lader, Lawrence. *Power on the Left: American Radical Movements Since 1946.* New York: W.W. Norton, 1979.

Lester, Julius and Mary Varela, ed. *To Praise Our Bridges.* Jackson, Miss.: KIPCO, 1967.

Leuchtenburg, William E. *A Troubled Feast: American Society Since 1945.* Boston: Little, Brown and Company, 1979.

Lewis, Anthony, and *The New York Times. Portrait of a Decade: The Second American Revolution*. New York: Random House, 1964.

Marcus, Robert D. and David Burner, ed. *America Since 1945*. New York: St. Martin's, 1977.

Raines, Howell. *My Soul Is Rested: Movement Days in the Deep South*. New York: Putnam's 1977.

Sewell, George A. *Mississippi Black History Makers*. Jackson: University Press of Mississippi, 1977.

Viorst, Milton. *Fire in the Streets*. New York: Touchstone, 1979.

White, Theodore H. *The Making of the President 1964*. New York: Mentor, 1966.

INDEX

About the Author

David Rubel is a writer and journalist whose work has appeared in such publications as the *Washington Post* and the *Boston Globe*. After graduating from Columbia University, he worked as a correspondent for the Pacific News Service, and then as a mathematics textbook editor. Currently, he is a children's book editor in New York City.

Text permissions:

From *Portrait of a Decade: The Second American Revolution* by Anthony Lewis and The New York Times. Copyright © 1964 by The New York Times Company. Reprinted by permission of Random House, Inc.

Transcript of Fannie Lou Hamer, Oral History Interview, Moorland-Spingarn Research Center, Howard University.

From *Hope and Dignity: Older Black Women of the South* by Emily Herring Wilson and Susan Weil Mulally. Reprinted by permission of Temple University Press.

From *To Praise Our Bridges*. Copyright © 1967 by Julius Lester and Mary Varela. Reprinted with permission of Julius Lester.

Reprinted with permission from *Sojourners*, Box 29272, Washington, D.C. 20017.

Picture Credits: AP/Wide World Photos: cover background, 10, 17, 62, 85, 91, 122; George Ballis: 12; Milwaukee Journal/Sentinel: cover portrait; Moorland-Spingarn Research Center: 119; Schomburg Center for Research in Black Culture, N.Y. Public Library, Astor, Lenox and Tilden Foundations: 15, 42, 47; UPI/Bettmann: 45, 113, 118.